Lyotard and Theology

PHILOSOPHY AND THEOLOGY SERIES

Other titles in the Philosophy and Theology series include:

Lyotard and Theology

Beyond the Christian master narrative of love

Lieven Boeve

BLOOMSBURY
LONDON • NEW DELHI • NEW YORK • SYDNEY

Bloomsbury T&T Clark

An imprint of Bloomsbury Publishing Plc

50 Bedford Square	1385 Broadway
London	New York
WC1B 3DP	NY 10018
UK	USA

www.bloomsbury.com

Bloomsbury is a registered trade mark of Bloomsbury Publishing Plc

First published 2014

British Library Cataloguing-in-Publication Data
A catalogue record for this book is available from the British Library.

ISBN: HB: 978-0-5670-3874-6
PB: 978-0-5672-8948-3
ePDF: 978-0-5671-7622-6
ePub: 978-0-5675-2311-2

Library of Congress Cataloging-in-Publication Data
Boeve, Lieven
Lyotard and Theology / Lieven Boeve p.cm
Includes bibliographic references and index.
ISBN 978-0-5670-3874-6 (hardcover) – ISBN 978-0-5672-8948-3 (pbk.)
2012045678

Typeset by Newgen Knowledge Works (P) Ltd., Chennai, India
Printed and bound in Great Britain

CONTENTS

PREFACE

For more than 20 years, the French philosopher Jean-François Lyotard has been one of the most important thinkers accompanying me as I theologize in a so-called postmodern context. I am, therefore, very happy to be able to bring together in this study some of the results of my theological engagement with one of the fathers of postmodern thinking. In this respect, references to my earlier work are mentioned in the Acknowledgements, which has been added as a postscript to this volume.

As a volume in the series *Philosophy and Theology*, which focuses on the impact contemporary philosophy has on the cause of theology, this book first and foremost presents the reader with an introduction to Lyotard's thought and its importance for contemporary theology. In this study, therefore, I first develop the main lines of Lyotard's philosophy of difference, in particular his own attempt to 'bear witness to the differend'. Afterwards I present how Lyotard's work challenges Christian theology and seriously questions its self-understanding. At the same time, I show how a critically productive engagement with Lyotard's intuitions and thinking patterns inspires theology to adequately respond to such criticism and challenge. Receiving Lyotard in theology, I will contend, helps one to develop strategies which go beyond the closing hegemony of the Christian master narrative of love.

In this respect, apart from being in its own right a monograph within a series, this study also serves to show some of the philosophical-theological intuitions and thinking patterns that undergird my earlier theological work. In the past I have published articles and books concerning the situation and prospects of Christian faith in a post-Christian and post-secular Europe, developing how the contextual interruption of the Christian tradition (through the processes of detraditionalization and pluralization) offers new and challenging opportunities for rediscovering the interruptive impulses at the heart of this tradition. I also tackled the issue of theological method in the present postmodern context in an attempt to move beyond the unproductive divide between modern correlationist and anti-modern (or postmodern) anti-correlationist theologies. In this endeavour, as well, the notion of interruption plays a crucial role, both in an epistemological and a political-theological respect. The present study will therefore make clear how this cultural-theological and methodological work is firmly anchored from within a theological and critically productive engagement with Lyotard's philosophy of difference and how the concept of interruption is thought of in line with his notion of the 'differend'. In the years to come, this book will be complemented by a more comprehensive study on the way in which thinkers of difference challenge theology in a critical-productive way to further its dialogue with the present-day context.

To conclude, I would like to express my gratitude to the members of the research groups 'Theology in a Postmodern Context' and 'Anthropos' at KU Leuven, which in many ways have supported the writing process of this book. In particular, I owe special thanks to Phillip Davis, for his comments and corrections on earlier versions of this text, and to Colby Dickinson and Bradford Manderfield for proofreading the final text. At the same time, I would like to thank the KU Leuven Research Fund (BOF), the Flemish Fund for Scientific Research (FWO), and the Faculty of Theology and Religious Studies at KU Leuven for their financial aid in support of research initiatives and projects, which, among others, has resulted in this book. Finally, I also wish to thank the editors and staff at Bloomsbury Publishing for including the present volume in this series.

Lieven Boeve

1

Introduction: On the non-reception of Lyotard in theology

In this introduction we will elaborate on how we understand the need for theological engagement with contemporary philosophy. Afterwards we first will discuss the remarkable non-reception of Lyotard in theology and, second, we will distinguish our approach from other approaches to do so. Finally, we will provide a concise outline of the present study. We will start, however, with a few biographical details regarding the author under consideration.

The father of the 'postmodern condition'

When Lyotard is cited today, it is usually in the context of his position that the 'grands récits', or 'métarécits', have lost their credibility and legitimacy. In 1979, in *La condition postmoderne*, with the intention of indicating the transformation he observed in Western society, Lyotard introduced the term 'postmodern' into philosophy, and, via philosophy, into many other domains.[1] Some ten years later, like many others associated with the postmodern turn, he was not happy with the frequent uncritical use of the term:

> The term postmodern has been used, badly rather than well if I judge by the results, to designate something of this transformation.[2]

On that occasion, he also stated that the expression 'réécrire la modernité', 'to rewrite modernity', should be used instead, being chosen above terminologies like 'postmodernity', 'postmodernism' and 'postmodern'.³ Later on, however, he seemed to use the word 'postmodern' again in quasi-unproblematic ways.⁴

Jean-François Lyotard was born in 1924 in Versailles, studied philosophy at the Sorbonne, and earned his doctorate in 1971, with the dissertation *Discours, Figure*, in which he criticized structuralism for its ahistorical and universalist features.⁵ In 1954, he joined 'Socialisme ou Barbarie', a critical French Marxist movement, which he left ten years later. He expressed his growing dissatisfaction with rigid Marxist theory in *Économie libidinale*, a work in which he engages the thought of both Karl Marx and Sigmund Freud and develops a philosophy of desire.⁶ He later turned his attention largely towards language pragmatics and aesthetic philosophy, and would seem to abandon this libidinal approach.⁷ In the meantime, after teaching in Constantine (French-occupied Algeria) in the early 1950s, he served as a teaching assistant at the Sorbonne. Later he lectured at the University of Nanterre and finally at the University of Paris VIII (Vincennes in Saint-Denis) until he retired in 1987. In the years before and after his retirement, he was invited to lecture as a visiting professor at many universities, especially in the United States. He died in 1998 and is buried in the Père Lachaise cemetery in Paris.

Theology in search of philosophy

For the purpose of this study, we will start our dealings with Lyotard's thought with *La condition postmoderne*, his groundbreaking description of the postmodern condition published in 1979, and the publications which followed this booklet. We will give special attention in this to his language pragmatics, where he develops his particular critique of modern master narratives, and, as an alternative, assigns to philosophy the task of bearing witness to the differend. We will show how his aesthetic philosophy of the sublime is a complement to, and in its own way, a proper attempt to 'bear witness to the differend'. Moreover, we will point to the critical force of his thinking of the differend, among other things in analysing capitalism. In as much as Lyotard considers Christianity as one more (very effective) master narrative, his criticism of master narratives is of direct concern to theology, challenging its attempts to reflect on the Christian faith in contextually plausible ways.

The latter is indeed the impulse from which we engage in this study of Lyotard. The plausibility of theological discourse is also determined by the context in which it operates. Theological tradition, as a movement through time, is co-constituted by the historical contexts in which it receives its shape and to which it addresses itself. Tradition therefore can be described as an *ongoing process of 'recontextualisation'*.[8] Often when contextual sensibilities shift, the dominant form of the tradition loses its plausibility, bringing forth experiences of alienation. It is only by renewing the relation between the received tradition and the changed context – resulting in new forms of tradition development – that such alienations can be overcome. As *fides quaerens intellectum*, faith in search of understanding, theology is called to be the reflective consciousness gained from within and accompanying such processes. For this purpose, philosophy has long been theology's preferred dialogue partner. As the reflective elucidation of contemporary sensibilities, philosophy (and the human sciences) confronts theology with a critical consciousness with regard to Christianity and the context itself, as well as providing contextually plausible vocabulary, analyses, thinking patterns and reflective strategies for theology to consciously undertake the theological task of recontextualization. It is from this perspective that we enter into conversation with Jean-François Lyotard.

The non-reception of Lyotard in theology

Despite Lyotard's influence on our understanding of the postmodern context and his criticism of the end of the modern master narratives, including the Christian one, it is remarkable that *his philosophy has not been seriously tackled by contemporary theological reflection*. This fact is all the more surprising since other thinkers of difference, such as Emmanuel Levinas, and especially Jacques Derrida, have received a far more prominent reception. In the 516 pages of *The Blackwell*

Companion to Postmodern Theology, for example, Lyotard is only mentioned 8 times, and not one of the 31 contributions is dedicated to an in-depth conversation with his thought. Derrida, on the other hand, is not only mentioned and quoted throughout the volume, but often serves also as the preferred conversation partner to tackle subjects such as the criticism of ontotheology, the 'gift', sacrifice, Christianity, naming God and negative theology, desire, dialogue, . . .[9]

Only a few exceptions can be found to the almost entirely absent reflection on Lyotard's philosophy in relation to the field of theology in academic study. In particular, Geoffrey Bennington has been interested in Lyotard's dealings with religion, more specifically with the distinction he makes between Christian and 'jew', and the repression of 'jewishness' by the Christian religion.[10] Also in monographs and collections on Lyotard's work, there is hardly an article or book in which the relation of Lyotard to Christianity and/or religion is studied in depth, and often depth; often this said relation is only commented upon in passing.[11] In books about the contribution of French philosophers to the philosophy of religion and theology, Lyotard is mainly the missing philosopher,[12] a notable exception being an article in the recently published *The Postmodern Saints of France*.[13] In this regard, I should also mention two minor studies which deal with Lyotard in a somewhat sustained manner, though neither work attempts to present a large-scale overview of (or introduction to) his relationship to theology as the present book intends. References here are to be made to James K. A. Smith's *Who's Afraid of Postmodernism? Taking Derrida, Lyotard, and Foucault to Church* and to Clayton Crockett's *A Theology of the Sublime*.[14] The only recent study to entertain a more in-depth perspective on Lyotard's work is Georges De Schrijver's *The Political Ethics of Jean-François Lyotard and Jacques Derrida*, though this work develops more of an ethical view on Lyotard's philosophy and less of a theological one.[15]

How to receive Lyotard into theology

When looking into Smith's conversation with the work of Lyotard, it is at least clear from the outset that he hopes to convince his rather hesitant (evangelical) audience that the 'devil does not come from Paris', and that one should not immediately and exclusively be afraid of the unholy trinity of postmodern thinking: said trinity being J. Derrida, J.-F. Lyotard and M. Foucault. He intends to demythologize postmodernism and to show how *postmodern insights may indeed be welcomed by Christians*: 'Something good *can* come out of Paris.'[16] What appears to be mutually exclusive at first glance, that is, postmodern thinking and orthodox Christianity, can form an alliance in the end. In this regard, he claims, vis-à-vis Lyotard, that:

> The assertion that postmodernity is 'incredulity toward metanarratives' is ultimately a claim to be affirmed by the church, pushing us to recover (a) the narrative character of Christian faith, rather than understanding it as a collection of ideas, and (b) the confessional nature of our narrative and the way in which we find ourselves in a world of competing narratives.[17]

Christians indeed should oppose metanarratives, even Christian ones, which legitimate themselves by universal reason so that their particularity is obfuscated. On the contrary, Christians should be sensitive to the particular narrative embeddedness of all claims of knowledge and truth. Therefore, says Smith, Lyotard does not criticize the narrative biblical ground of Christian faith, but the forgetting of this when arguing for Christian truth claims through universal reason.[18] The outcome of the postmodern criticism of modern metanarratives is a plurality of discourses and narratives, and, Smith adds, it is up to us to consider whether we understand this new situation 'as a new Babel or a new Pentecost'.[19]

It will be clear from our study that we share these conclusions, but *not in the same way as Smith* intends them. For him, and in line with other thinkers from the Radical Orthodoxy movement,[20] the three postmodern thinkers he deals with all invite Christians to look backwards to 'premodern ways of knowing, being and doing', and to retrieve thick traditions which are unaffected by modernity. Indeed, Lyotard only serves Smith's cause by demythologizing modern rationality as but one more myth or narrative while simultaneously opening up space for Christians to engage their own narrative sources for the purpose of developing their own Christian philosophy.

My point is not to suggest that Lyotard's analysis concretely helps to understand Christian faith; in other words, I am not arguing that we look to Lyotard for assistance in understanding Christian faith commitments. Rather, Christian thinkers should find in Lyotard's critique of metanarratives and autonomous reason an ally that opens up the space for a radically Christian witness in the postmodern world. [...] Lyotard relativises (secular) philosophy's claim to autonomy and so grants the legitimacy of a philosophy that grounds itself in Christian faith. [. . .] The exclusion of faith from the public square is a modern agenda; postmodernity should signal new openings and opportunities for Christian witness in the broad market place of ideas.[21]

In sum, Smith's conversation with Lyotard stops when the field whereupon the Christian narrative is to be told is opened up again by deconstructing the massive hegemony of modern rationality. Postmodernity here seems literally understood as 'after modernity' (whereas Lyotard would opt for 'rewriting modernity'). Lyotard serves the goal of allowing Christians to make their claims to truth in the same ways as others, including moderns, do. In this regard, and with Smith's use of an old notion, *philosophia praeparatio evangelica*: Lyotard only sets the stage for a Christian philosophy anchored within the Christian narrative to be developed in its own right.[22]

We must be careful not to continue to propagate that witness in modernist ways: by attempting our own rationalist demonstrations of the truth of Christian faith and then imposing such on a pluralist culture. [. . .] While [a new Christian] apologetics will be an *un*apologetics, it will at the same time be characterized by faithful storytelling, not demonstration. It must be kerygmatic and charismatic: proclaiming the story of the gospel in the power of the Spirit.[23]

Smith here joins the post-liberal theological approach (as exemplified in the work of George Lindbeck and Stanley Hauerwas), which bets on narrative-internal forms of rationality and legitimation of truth. Being a Christian is first and foremost, from this perspective, living the story in word and deed on a daily basis.

This is, however, not the way we will proceed in this book. Of course, we also appreciate the reception Smith gives to Lyotard's contribution to theology, as well as his retrieval of narrative and witness in daily life. But whereas Smith limits this contribution to a first stage, we intend *to push our conversation with Lyotard one step further*. There are two reasons to do so. First of all, within the theological tradition to which I belong, the issue of faith and reason, and thus of the dialogue between philosophy and theology, does not stop at setting the stage for a merely internal theological storytelling, but affects the very way in which this story will be told. In as much as earlier theological approaches, such as the ones of Augustine, Thomas Aquinas, Karl Rahner, etc., were constructed through intense conversations with the philosophies of their times, so also a contemporary theological recontextualization will be challenged by today's philosophical critical consciousness. Moreover, as these examples show, such a conversation will not only help to critically evaluate theology as it has been practised so far, but will, at the same time, contribute to the elaboration of a specifically contemporary reflective Christian critical consciousness, striving after both contextual plausibility and theological legitimacy. In such a conversation philosophy not only helps to set the stage (*praeparatio evangelica*), but assists theology's continuous project of developing a 'faith seeking understanding' (*ancilla theologiae*).

Second, Smith seems to conclude that Lyotard's contribution is one of setting the field free from modern rationalities so as to allow for the telling of a plurality of discourses and narratives (including the Christian narrative). From our analysis it will become clear that allowing for plurality is neither the first nor the most important point made by Lyotard. Plurality is not Lyotard's starting point; rather, it is conflict: indeed, there are a plurality of discourses and narratives, but only one can be told at a time. Plurality involves conflict. It is from this starting point, then, that Lyotard develops his own thinking of difference, or better, of *heterogeneity*, particularly by analysing what happens in a 'differend'. It is this focus on heterogeneity that fuels his criticism of modern, but also of postmodern, master narratives.

Rather than as a model allowing for plurality, it is this challenge of heterogeneity, and its event-character, which will inspire our own proposal in this study. From this it will become clear that, like all narratives, Christian discourse-internal dealings with truth all too often tend to forget about heterogeneity, unless they find ways, from within their own discourses, to bear witness to that which is never to be contained in a discourse but challenges it continuously. The task we assign ourselves is, therefore, to find ways to open up the Christian narrative to heterogeneity, and to look for opportunities to make such thinking patterns theologically fruitful when considering God's relationship with humanity in creation and history.

In summary, the opportunity offered by Lyotard's philosophy consists not only in allowing us to do theology once again, but will also bear upon the way in which we engage in theological recontextualization today. At the same time, and in view of the non-reception of Lyotard in theology, I hope to make it clear that interacting with Lyotard presents theology with more than simply an encounter with another thinker of difference; it also offers particularly fruitful starting points for theologizing today, maybe even more fruitful than the use of thinkers like Derrida.

Outline of the present study

To conclude, I will briefly present the outline of this book. As already mentioned, the first chapters of the book offer a concise presentation of Jean-François Lyotard's thinking of difference. We will introduce Lyotard's critical postmodern thought, both in its language pragmatic approach (Chapter 2, on the differend) and its aesthetic form (Chapter 3, on the sublime). We will illustrate this through an analysis of his criticisms of capitalism (Chapter 4). Chapter 5 presents us with a further elaboration of Lyotard's analysis of Christianity as a master narrative. From the following chapters onward, we engage Lyotard's critical thinking with respect to its reception in theology. In Chapter 6, therefore, we will look with Lyotard for openings within the Christian master narrative which might offer opportunities to make room for naming God in non-hegemonic ways. We will do so in reference to the so-called theological turn, or the turn to religion, in contemporary continental philosophy. In this regard, we will propose the possibility of a Christian open narrative which attempts to overcome the hegemonic features that continuously threaten the narrative genre (and especially the master narrative). In Chapter 7, we will further explore the language pragmatic plausibility of what would constitute an open narrative and apply our insights both language pragmatically and theologically with regard to a Christian open narrative. In Chapter 8, we inquire into the philosophical-theological plausibility of our reception of Lyotard in theology, and by doing so, offer a broader reflection on the more general issue of the critical-productive relationship between theology and philosophy through a case study. Finally, in Chapters 9 and 10, we illustrate in two ways how our theological conversation with Lyotard offers new and inspiring possibilities, first, with regard to thinking the Christian sacramental understanding of history and world in relation to God, and, second, in readjusting the critical-constructive argumentative strength of late-modern political theology (J. B. Metz). In the conclusion, we rehearse some of the main insights of this book and offer some prospects for further research.

2

Philosophy in the postmodern condition: On the incredulity of modern master narratives and bearing witness to the differend

Introduction: The postmodern condition

In 1979, in *La condition postmoderne*, Lyotard wrote for the first time that the 'master narratives' ('grand récits', 'métarécits') have lost their credibility and legitimacy. This statement summarized his investigation into the *transformation of the status of knowledge* as the transition to a post-industrial society and a postmodern culture.[1] In the current era, he concluded, knowledge is no longer legitimated by traditional pre-modern narrative discourses, nor is it legitimated by modern grand narratives. Regarding the latter, Lyotard distinguished between two types of modern grand narratives: the philosophical-speculative and the political grand narrative. The first takes its form in German Idealism as a unifying meta-discourse wherein the speculative grand narrative legitimizes our knowledge about nature, society and the state by integrating it within the development of the life of the Spirit. The second political narrative of legitimation puts knowledge in service to the emancipation of humanity, that is, in the service of freedom. Examples hereof are liberalism and Marxism. The freedom to be acquired takes shape in the law, which is an expression of the will of the people. Knowledge then functions within the framework of this imperative.

In the postmodern condition, according to Lyotard, these modern metanarratives have lost their plausibility. Knowledge is currently legitimated by its *performativity*. Knowledge is first and foremost characterized by the fact that it works, that it makes things possible. The optimization of its performativity is realized through a constant revolutionizing of the existing scientific discourse, breaking it open with newness. Progress as such is helped along not by the homology of experts (which operates within a single paradigm) but by the *paralogy of inventors* (which interrupts existing paradigms). Therefore, paradigms are to be continually broken open, rules of the game to be adjusted and games to be changed. The object of science is formed not by what is already known and familiar, but by the unknown and the unfamiliar.[2]

For Lyotard, it is particularly interesting to apply these insights regarding science to the social domain, because, in Western societies, whoever decides about the truth is often the one who also decides about what is good and just. Science, ethics and politics go hand-in-hand. Analogous to his reflections on science, then, Lyotard affirms that society as well – and its search for justice – cannot be described exhaustively as a system. Although the diminution of social complexity and the streamlining of individual aspirations by the computerized media would seem to result in an exceptionally performative system, such strategies will fail. Indeed, scientific pragmatics teaches that paralogy shatters and changes the state of affairs. Whoever wants to prevent rupture and change is drawn to a science based purely on power, protecting the system and the positions of those investing power. Such strategies in the end result in terror. The same is true in social pragmatics. In the social realm, a diversity of language games exists that likewise can no longer be contained in one grand encompassing narrative. According to Lyotard, this situation disables Habermas' model of consensus-oriented communicative rationality.[3] In order for this rationality to function, all concerned parties would first have to reach an agreement concerning the meta-linguistic rules governing all language games, and second, they would have to assume that rational communicative praxis necessarily leads or should lead to consensus. The heterogeneity of language games and their rules, however, and the possibility of dissent, make such obligatory striving for consensus dubious. Habermas' proposal in fact still resembles the strategies of the grand narratives of emancipation, in which a universal subject moves to freedom via a universally shared consensual knowledge. For Lyotard, however, *the question of justice* is no longer able to lean upon such a consensus-oriented model, but should radically start from *dissensus*. Only a local consensus is still possible – that is, one limited in space and time.

After its publication, this booklet received a huge response. According to the publisher's comments in one of Lyotard's following publications, *Le postmoderne expliqué aux enfants*, its author was accused of irrationalism, neo-conservatism, intellectual terrorism, naive liberalism, nihilism, cynicism and other epithets.[4] In turn, he himself argued that many of these criticisms, such as those of Jürgen Habermas and Richard Rorty, did not do justice to the nature of the document.[5] At the time, his answer to these criticisms was also already underway: in the introduction to *La condition postmoderne* Lyotard had already announced a more fundamental work that would reflect more philosophically upon what was at stake in the discussion.

> The philosopher at least can console himself with the thought that the formal and pragmatic analysis of certain philosophical and ethico-political discourses of legitimation, which underlies the report [*The Postmodern Condition*], will subsequently see the light of day. The report will have served to introduce that analysis from a somewhat sociologizing slant, one that truncates but at the same time situates it.[6]

This book appeared in 1983, entitled *Le différend*.[7] In taking up the perspective of language pragmatics, Lyotard further developed herein the way in which justice is related to dealing with dissensus as an alternative to a too simplistic consensus thinking. Another important publication in the wake of *Le différend*, and dealing with the same issues, was *Judicieux dans le différend*.[8] In the years following, Lyotard published a few anthologies in which he gathered contributions discussing the postmodern condition from very different perspectives: *Tombeau de l'intellectuel et autres papiers*,[9] the already cited *Le postmoderne expliqué aux enfants*, *L'inhumain: Causeries sur le temps* and *Moralités postmodernes*. Also worth mentioning are *L'enthousiasme: La critique kantienne de l'histoire, Leçons sur l'Analytique du sublime* and *Peregrinations: Law, Form, Event*.[10]

In what follows, we will draw on the language pragmatics of Jean-François Lyotard as they have helped him to develop his postmodern critical analysis of master narratives and to foster his own 'bearing witness to the differend'.[11] We will accordingly make clear how he deals with irresolvable conflicts, especially with the forgetfulness of otherness which is at stake in such conflicts. Lyotard shows how these conflicts are to be analysed as differends, which tend to be resolved as litigations by the discourse genre that wins the struggle. By so doing he offers a profound criticism of the mastery which hegemonic discourses, and especially master narratives, may exert on the 'differend', undoing it of its unpresentable otherness through the act of naming it and subjugating it to the logic of the ruling discourse. At the same time, Lyotard makes exemplary efforts to respect the differend, to bear witness to the event of heterogeneity which accompanies all discourse, and, by so doing, attempts to open up new possibilities to think difference, otherness and heterogeneity without falling back into the patterns of a grand narrative. In the next chapter, we will also point out how Lyotard's dealings with postmodern aesthetics have led him to very similar reflections, demonstrating an analogy between his aesthetic and language pragmatic work.

Basic categories of Lyotard's language pragmatics: Phrases, phrase regimens and discourse genres

Lyotard situates his philosophical reflections primarily in a dialogue with Ludwig Wittgenstein and Immanuel Kant. With the Wittgenstein of the *Philosophical Investigations* he shares a concern with language and the heterogeneity of language games, and thus attests to the linguistic turn in recent philosophy.[12] In Kant, Lyotard discerns the traits of a philosophy that succeeds in distinguishing between different forms of rationality while, at the same time, indicating their limits. Moreover he is interested in Kant's elaborations on the 'transitions' between these different forms of rationality – which Kant was after in his *Kritik der Urteilskraft* – and as expressed in Lyotard's language pragmatics: the linking of phrases.[13]

In this first section we will therefore introduce the basic categories of Lyotard's language pragmatics: phrases, phrase regimens, discourse genres, phrase universe and event. As we will see in the following sections, these categories not only enable him to re-describe what is at stake in philosophy after the linguistic turn, but also to critically engage the postmodern condition after the demise of the modern master narratives.

Lyotard's criticism of master narratives issues forth from the way in which he analyses what 'happens' in language. He begins this analysis with the observation that first there is a *phrase* ('phrase'). A phrase happens. After all, 'there can be no doubt that it happens, because it happens that you doubt' (D104).[14] And there is an unending multitude of phrases residing simply there as 'given'. Examples of such phrases are: 'the door is closed'; 'once upon a time there was a girl who always wore a red cap'; 'forgive us our sins'; 'that will be a hundred euros'; 'close the door', etc. Each of these phrases belongs to a *phrase regimen* ('régime de phrases'). The latter consists of a number of rules which determine the forming of suitable phrases according to the phrase regimen (D30).[15] In other words, a particular phrase can always be catalogued, according to its regimen, as descriptive, interrogative, prescriptive, declarative, exclamatory and so on. Moreover, a phrase from one phrase regimen cannot be translated as such into another phrase regimen (D78).[16]

Now a 'happened' phrase, and this is crucial, is always followed by a new phrase. To one phrase, another phrase is always linked. In this regard, even silence can be a phrase. However, although the linking between phrases is necessary, the nature of the linking is fundamentally *contingent*. In principle, whatever phrase happens can realize this linking with a former phrase (D136). A descriptive phrase, for example, is not necessarily followed by a prescriptive phrase (D166, 178). The phrase 'it is warm in here' is not necessarily followed by the request 'can you open the door, please?', or the command 'open the door!', but may be followed by phrases such as 'it is cold outside', or 'that is not true', or 'the phrase "it is warm in here" is a descriptive phrase'.

The linking of (or passage from) one phrase to another phrase is regulated under the framework of a *discourse genre* ('genre de discours'). A genre of discourse is that which is at the service of a specific goal, and through which the linking of a phrase with a specific other phrase is formed within the strategy of the genre of discourse in order to achieve that goal (D40). In other words, a genre of discourse forms a unity of rules that connect heterogeneous phrases to each other with the aim of realizing a specific finality (D147). Examples of discourse genres include argumentation, narrative, seduction, rhetoric, pedagogy, humour, prayer and so on. The phrase 'it is warm in here' may accordingly function very differently in a seductive setting than in a linguistics class.

The phrase itself occurs in a 'universe of names' (D47–93, 133), and extends a *phrase universe* that is not given in advance but is presented along with the phrase, in the occurrence itself of the phrase. This universe contains four elements or 'instances': the addressor (the one who utters the phrase); the addressee to whom the phrase is directed; the referent (what is at stake); and the meaning (what is said about that which is at stake). The phrase joins these four elements together, each of which may be plural: there can indeed be various meanings, various addressees . . . These instances do not have to be made explicit in the phrase (D25, 111) and may shift according to the nature of the phrase linked to it. The phrase universe of 'it is very warm in here', as mentioned already, significantly changes when linked to the discourse genre of seduction rather than the genre of a pedagogical discourse.

In short the occurrence of a phrase is an *event*. The nature of the phrase to happen is thereby not predetermined. Neither its content nor addressor nor referent is imposed (or can be imposed) by the preceding phrase. There is thus a kind of 'relative nothingness' between the latter and the phrase to follow. In other words, a happened phrase opens an expectation onto an event to come: 'is it happening?' ('arrive-t-il?'). The only thing which is certain is that a phrase will follow.

It is necessary *that* something happens (the event), but *what* happens (the phrase, its meaning, object, interlocutors) is never necessary – the necessity of contingency or, if you like, the being of nonbeing.[17]

In the 'third note on Kant' in *Le différend*, taken up again in an extended way in *L'enthousiasme*,[18] Lyotard offers the image of an *archipelago* to clarify his view on language. The diverse phrase regimens are like islands, he comments. The series of physically separated and mutually distinguished islands symbolize the irrefutable diversity of phrase regimes. But links between the islands over the sea are possible. What island one is travelling to and with what intention one travels to a particular island, in principle, remain fundamentally open. Once at sea, however, it is obvious that one ultimately arrives at an island. It is then the goal by which one travels from one island to the other which determines the destination and the way one approaches this destination, and these goals may be very different. A commercial expedition approaches an island in a different manner than a cruise ship, let alone a war fleet.[19]

Conflict and injustice within language: Differends and litigations

Since the linking of two phrases is a contingent event, a conflict will inevitably break out concerning every happened phrase over the linkage of the phrase that follows. In essence, this conflict is a conflict that exists between discourse genres. That is, one and the same phrase can act in several discourse genres, but there is always only one other phrase which can follow. It is the discourse that wins the conflict that ultimately determines the nature of this phrase and closes off the expectation ('is it happening?') opened up by the preceding phrase. The winning discourse genre defines the phrase which is linked, and fills in the 'relative nothingness' in-between the passage from one phrase to the other. It is this conflict between discourse genres over the linking of phrases that constitutes a *differend* ('différend'), and which is to be distinguished from a litigation ('litige').[20] With every linking a differend arises since the event and the phrase to happen are claimed by various discourse genres, and there is no pre-given overarching and binding rule that prescribes the way in which the linking should be realized. On the other hand, Lyotard describes a *litigation* as a conflict that is immediately decided in the idiom of one of the competing discourse genres. In a litigation the 'relative nothingness' between two phrases is forgotten. The ruling discourse genre regulates the linking – in order to achieve its own goal – as if no fundamental contingency would be given with respect to the nature of the phrase to be linked. A litigation thus undoes the linking of its event character (D188).

To comprehend Lyotard's undertaking, one must consider this *irreducible conflict* as the fundamental characteristic of the way in which language operates. A happened phrase opens up an expectation, which is consequently closed by a subsequent phrase. Because, however, no supreme rule is given to determine the nature of this following phrase, and thus a plurality of phrases potentially present themselves to complete the linkage, an irresolvable conflict arises for which no ultimate solution is available. The choice for one particular phrase necessarily excludes the actualization of the other phrases. The triumph of one phrase implies the defeat of all the others. Plurality cannot be radically respected, nor can the legitimate claims of any other phrase (or discourse genre) to realize a linkage. The accompanying feeling is one of powerlessness and unavoidable *injustice*. The ruling discourse hegemonically arranges the linkage as if no real expectation was opened up, as if no event was to happen (D188). As such, the other parties cannot tell their story, their complaint is not heard and their witness is not relevant because it is always set forward in an 'unsuitable' idiom (D12). Denied the possibility of speaking, they are condemned to silence (D13–16). What is a litigation for the ruling discourse is experienced by the others as a differend, ultimately then as a form of injustice.

Lyotard's most prominent example of such a differend, with which he opens *Le différend*, is the differend experienced by the survivors of Auschwitz at the statement of the French negationist Faurisson,[21] specifically when the latter claimed that these survivors cannot sufficiently demonstrate the existence of the gas chambers. In reality, the existence of a Nazi gas chamber cannot actually be proven, since not a single victim can testify to having seen it in operation: whoever testifies has not really been in the gas chamber; whoever has actually entered the gas chamber can no longer testify to it (D2). What makes one a victim is that he or she can no longer testify to the evil inflicted on them: evil takes away that possibility (D7–9), and condemns one to silence.[22]

In every conflict, Lyotard therefore ultimately recognizes a *linguistic* conflict – because it is already always stated in language (D12, 21), and must therefore be dealt with from a linguistic perspective.

> The question of the differend is not anthropological but linguistic. No matter how they appear, differends are not about the satisfaction of interests or 'human' passions.[23]

With this connection, Lyotard also redefines the notion of *politics*. The political is not a discourse genre, but the playground where different discourse genres are at work. Politics exists by the grace of the phrases, linkages, expectations, and 'relative nothingness' (D190). The question 'which phrase is to be linked?' is indeed fundamentally a political question. Considering that – on the political field – differends are procedurally regulated as litigations (one genre always wins), the goal of politics can never be to realize the good, only to work for the lesser of all possible evils (D187): to bear witness to the occurrence of every new phrase and thus to every new differend. Conversely, a politics that coercively attempts to regulate the battlefield of the linkages of phrases ascribes hegemony to one particular genre of discourse (D200). It identifies itself with one particular genre of discourse and forgets that each new phrase is an event, thus forgetting the differend itself. It imposes its authority by favouring the rules of one genre of discourse, and, by doing so, becomes hegemonic (D199). Politics can do so, for example, through myths, as with primitive people; or through technical discourse, as in the industrial revolution; or through economic discourse, as in a capitalist society.

The discourse genre of the narrative, and the modern master narrative

The *narrative* ('récit') is a special discourse genre, because in this genre the heterogeneity of phrase regimens and of discourse genres is most easily forgotten. The narrative exhaustively 're'tells the differend and

situates it within its own finality. Within the presented totality, the
differend comes to its end because it is stripped of its jolting event-
character (D230). Or as Lyotard tersely states: because a narrative
is self-enclosed, one cannot step out of it. Questions about extra-
narrative legitimation are of no significance. Lyotard illustrates this
with the myths of the Latin American Cashinahua Indians: through
a plurality of small narratives, each narrating about a founding past,
the members of the tribe are integrated into their universe of names,
in essence their cultural world.[24] Each Cashinahua receives his or
her name and identity from these stories; and it is only through this
name that he or she can be a listener of stories, and later become the
one to pass them on. The question of the narrator's authority and
of the worth of his or her story is answered through the story itself,
something to which the narrator owes his or her name and identity.
The power of the story furnishes the legitimacy.

> [The story] encompasses the multiplicity of families of phrases
> and possible genres of discourse; it envelops every name; it is
> always actualizable and always has been; both diachronic and
> parachronic, it secures mastery over time and therefore over
> life and death. Narrative is authority itself. It authorizes an
> infrangible *we*, outside of which there is only *they*.[25]

The event can only 'happen' within these rigid frameworks: the
'relative nothingness' between two phrases is immediately qualified
through the rule of the story. Each phrase to happen is a suitable
phrase, fitting to the realization of the finality of the story. The
differend always appears as a litigation.

A special kind of narrative is the *(modern) master narrative*. In
the case of this latter discourse genre, it is no longer through a set
of small stories that the universe of names is given shape, but by
one encompassing grand narrative of history. In *Le postmoderne
expliqué aux enfants*, Lyotard distinguishes between the following
master narratives:

> [. . .] the Christian narrative of the redemption of original sin
> through love; the *Aufklärer* narrative of emancipation from this
> ignorance and servitude through knowledge and egalitarianism;
> the speculative narrative of the realization of the universal Idea
> through the dialectic of the concrete; the Marxist narrative of

emancipation from exploitation and alienation through the socialization of work; and the capitalist narrative of emancipation from poverty through techno-industrial development.[26]

Further developing Lyotard's indications, we can roughly distinguish between *four characteristics* with regard to modern master narratives: on the one hand *two narrative* characteristics which master narratives share with (pre-modern) mythical narratives, and, on the other hand, *two modern* characteristics which distinguish them from the latter. What is most specific for master narratives, in this regard, is that they can be analysed as hegemonic discourses which are regulated by an 'Idea'.

The first of the narrative characteristics is the master narrative's *cognitive claim*. Like myths, master narratives claim to be able to describe reality truthfully and thereby betray a cognitive pretension: they claim to present reality as it is. The second narrative characteristic is the master narrative's *totalizing power*. Master narratives are closed hegemonic discourses: they regulate the linking of phrases immediately, in a quasi-automatic way, and subordinate all other discourse genres. By doing so, they have no trouble linking descriptive and prescriptive phrases together (thus making so-called is-ought statements). They legitimate institutions, social life, politics, ethics, legislation, ideology, etc. Moreover, the hegemony of the narrative genre of discourse does not allow for external questions regarding its legitimacy, and thus enables the narrative to escape the problem of its own legitimacy.

What distinguishes master narratives from pre-modern mythologies are their two modern characteristics. First, modernity's narrative structure no longer consists of many small stories which legitimate the culture as from a foundational beginning. Rather it is a *grand narrative of history* which legitimates itself through its *finality*. Second, a master narrative has *universal pretentions*. For that reason, it wipes out all particular names and claims to speak of, and on behalf of, the whole of 'humanity' (D221). Technically speaking, all particular instances of the phrase universe (addressor, addressee, referent and meaning) are in principle to be universalized: the universal addressor, addressee, etc. have then outgrown the position of local narrator, listener, etc. (D226).[27]

It is especially the observation that master narratives are hegemonic (and thus degenerated) *discourses regulated by an Idea*, which largely accounts for the difference between these narratives and pre-modern mythologies. For the notion of 'Idea' ('Idée'), Lyotard refers to Kant's approach in which Ideas have a conceptual function, as they assist in conceiving reality through the mediation of a universal concept.[28] It is such an Idea which is at play in master narratives with regard to all four characteristics. As regards the two modern characteristics of the master narrative: (a) this Idea then is the finality, the goal or end, which dominates and legitimizes the narrative – by striving after its realization, it turns the narrative into a grand narrative of history; and (b) it universalizes the instances of the phrase universe by simultaneously taking in *all* instances. As regards the two narrative characteristics: (c) the Idea claims to present reality as it is, and (d) regulates linkages in an exclusive manner. An important issue regarding an Idea, however, is its unpresentability, which is completely overlooked by master narratives. Because Ideas only have a conceptual and not a cognitive function in language, assisting in conceiving reality through the mediation of a universal concept, the referent of such an Idea cannot as such be presented, but can only be attested to in indirect symbolic presentations, in signs (of history, 'signe d'histoire'). However, in a master narrative, a cognitive value is attributed to such signs of history, rather than taking them as symbolic, indirect presentations of the Idea at stake in the narrative. These signs, then, are no longer seen as indirect attestations but as direct presentations: that is, as examples or proofs.

Lyotard's example of *Marxism*, as the *hegemonic discourse of the Idea of the emancipated proletariat*, may illustrate the way in which a hegemonic discourse of an Idea works. (a) From a Marxist perspective, the finality of history is the realization of the Idea: an emancipated proletariat, the classless society. (b) This Idea also universalizes the instances by absorbing them into itself: the referent of the Idea (the proletariat) is identical with the addressor (the proletariat) who prescribes communism (the emancipated proletariat) to the addressee (also the proletariat). (c) Marxism makes the cognitive claim that it – and it alone – is able to represent the dynamics of reality according to the logic of dialectical-materialism. (d) Finally, all linkages are necessarily regulated by the Idea, and are compulsorily enforced on the basis of the narrative's power to describe reality and to achieve the Idea's plan (i.e. descriptive and prescriptive phrases are quasi-automatically linked).

Whoever stands outside of the narrative does not possess class-consciousness; whoever steps outside is a counter-revolutionary. Because the referent of the Idea of the emancipated proletariat is, after all, not presentable as such, its reality was indeed attested to by a sign of history, though it was taken as a cognitive indication rather than as a symbolic presentation. As such, the enthusiasm and high hopes of the working class were considered as proof for the validity of the Marxist way towards emancipation.[29] Moreover, in communist regimes, the referent (and thus also the addressor . . .) has been further identified with the Party, thus making the Idea of the proletariat directly presentable and forgetting its unpresentable nature.[30]

The *liberal master narrative of emancipation* can also be analysed as a hegemonic discourse narrative of an Idea. (a) According to this narrative, the ultimate goal of history is the realization of the freedom of the subject. (b) Moreover, the Idea of freedom universalizes the possible particular instances by taking all of them in: humanity is called to be a free humanity and to realize freedom as a free humanity. Particular instances of emancipation are thus taken up and rid of their particular shape along the universal road to freedom. (c) With regard to the cognitive pretension of the grand narrative of the Idea of freedom, the essence of history is that it is on its way to freedom and that freedom will finally be realized: that is, reality comes to its fulfilment in freedom. In this light, historical processes are evaluated, rejected or recommended. (d) In the latter case, this master narrative's hegemonic way of dealing with differends becomes clear. The Idea of freedom is the ultimate criterion by which all is measured and to which everything is subordinated. Whatever has the potential of freedom within itself, becomes normative; whatever goes against freedom is intolerable and should be extinguished. Whoever questions the project of freedom stands outside of human history and undermines his or her own capacity to criticize this project, because legitimate criticism presupposes precisely the Idea of freedom, which is rejected.

Finally, Lyotard sees the characteristics of the master narrative as a hegemonic discourse of an Idea also present in the procedure of linking phrases via the *speculative genre*, and for which Hegel's philosophy is the example par excellence. It is the Idea of the absolute Self (a) of which its realization is the finality of history, (b) which takes on the instances of the phrase universe, (c) describes reality as it is, and

(d) hegemonically regulates the linking of phrases. All links between phrases function within a rigid scheme of necessity. Differends do not have a chance. The event is 'systematically' established.[31]

It is precisely this *forgetfulness of the differend* (of the event, the expectation, the 'relative nothingness') that produced the hegemonic, totalitarian and oppressive features of the master narrative as a discourse of an Idea. Master narratives are therefore degenerated discourses of the Idea, where the Idea as Idea – that is, as an unpresentable general concept – is not respected.

The postmodern discrediting of the modern grand narratives

In the postmodern condition, modern master narratives suffer from *incredulity because they have not been able to live up to the promises they announced*. Instead of realizing the humanity, freedom and emancipation they promised, they brought rather totalitarianism and terror. They were shattered by counterexamples: the speculative doctrine that everything that is real is rational, and vice versa, was shattered by Auschwitz;[32] the historical-materialistic doctrine that every proletarian is a communist, and vice versa, was ruined in Berlin (1953), Budapest (1956), Czechoslovakia (1968), Poland (1980) and, later, in the fall of the Berlin wall (1989); the doctrine of liberal parliamentarianism, that politics works for and through the people, received a severe blow in May 1968; the various versions of economic liberalism which supposed that the free market of supply and demand would bring well-being for all, were smashed to smithereens by the economic crises of 1911, 1929, 1974–79. The so-called realization of promises brought nothing but blood and misery.[33]

Modern developments no longer seem to contribute to the future fulfilment of the announced reign of freedom and can still hardly be legitimated

> by promising emancipation for humanity as a whole. This promise has not been kept. It was broken, not because it was forgotten, but because development itself makes it impossible to keep. The new illiteracy, the impoverishment of people in the South and the Third World, unemployment, the tyranny of

opinion and the prejudices then echoed in the media, the law that performance is the measure of the good – all this is due not to a lack of development, but to development itself. This is why we would no longer dream of calling it progress.[34]

Hence, Lyotard is convinced that the *modern project* is not unfinished and abandoned, as Habermas opines, but *destroyed*.[35] This project can no longer be started again, but has realized its own self-destruction.

For Lyotard, in the postmodern context, the incredulity of the master narratives goes hand-in-hand with the discovery of their real nature as exaggerated *hegemonic discourses of an Idea* that adheres to illegitimate universal and cognitive pretensions. They are degenerated because in them the Idea as Idea is not respected and its unpresentable nature is forgotten. As should be clear, for Lyotard it is not the discourse of the Idea itself which is at stake here (this certainly has its place within the plurality of other discourses), but rather its hegemonic regulative aspiration (a) to be *the* narrative that defines the goal of history; (b) to encompass whatever happens through the universalization of the instances; (c) to pronounce the truth in an all-encompassing way for all, and (d) to quasi-automatically regulate the linkages of (e.g. prescriptive to descriptive) phrases, thereby authoritatively including or excluding other possible phrases and genres.

The postmodern sign of history and the task of philosophy: Bearing witness to the differend

In the postmodern condition, master narratives are unmasked as discourses that regulate the linking of phrases as 'of necessity', when, in principle, they are open and contingent. Today, such a quasi-automatic reduction of a differend to a litigation is no longer tolerable and is accompanied by a indefinable feeling which Lyotard considers the *sign of history* of our times, an attestation to the end of the modern master narratives.

As already indicated above, following Kant, Lyotard considers that an Idea points to a general concept to which the referent cannot be directly presented. Only *indirect, symbolic presentations*, or signs, are appropriate. Such signs are especially important for Ideas of the political-historical field. Such a sign of history succeeds in evoking an Idea in the historical arena without yet proving it, or without attributing a cognitive value to it. Kant recognized such a sign in the enthusiasm that the French Revolution released among its spectators, and saw therein an indication that the goal of human history is the Idea of freedom.[36] As already mentioned, modern master narratives often forgot the indirect, symbolic character of these signs, using them as direct presentations of the referent of the Idea ruling their hegemonic discourses. However, as Lyotard remarks elsewhere, one should be cautious in the discernment of signs and their specific nature:

> A war of liberation does not indicate that humanity is continuing to emancipate itself. Nor does the opening of new markets indicate humanity's increasing wealth.[37]

At the end of the twentieth century, Lyotard wrote in *Le différend* (1983) that spectators perceive a feeling of *sadness* that is in fact a sense of the gap between the reality of the time and the promises of the discourses of the Idea, a feeling that accompanies an awareness of the radicalized heterogeneity of the genres of discourse (D256–57). In *L'enthousiasme* (1986), Lyotard no longer designated this feeling. He spoke rather of a feeling of not only

> the irremediable gap between an Idea and whatever presents itself in order to 'realize' it [that] would be felt, but also the gap between various phrase families and their respective legitimate presentations.[38]

It is the feeling occasioned by events like Auschwitz, Budapest, May 1968 and others. Perhaps we can speak of the feeling of a gap – a split attesting to an Idea that has as its goal precisely an adherence to a plurality of heterogeneous finalities: the *Idea of heterogeneity*.

> For it is not only the Idea of *an* end that is pointed out by our feeling, but already the Idea that this end consists in the formation and free exploration of Ideas, that this end is the beginning of the infinity of heterogeneous finalities.[39]

Expressed differently, it concerns the feeling of the *impossible phrase*.[40] The phrase fulfilling the link always fails in expressing the Idea. In *Moralités postmodernes* (1993), he again designates the feeling as melancholy.[41]

What is the *role of philosophy* in all this? Is it narrating the master narrative of the end of the master narratives, 'le grand récit du déclin des grands récits' (D182)?[42] Lyotard does not think so. The philosophical genre, in Lyotard's view, can best be described as a contemporary version of Kant's tribunal of reason, of critical philosophy – with the difference, to be sure, that it is not the Idea of freedom in a philosophy of the subject that functions in the background, but that it proceeds within the framework of a philosophy of phrases. Philosophy, therefore, first and foremost analyses phrase regimens and genres of discourse; it points to rules of formation and linking prescriptions, investigates phrases and validates them from the perspective of these rules. Philosophy, however, must especially keep open the heterogeneity of the diverse phrases and genres to which the linking bears witness (and this, for example, against Kant who, with the help of the Idea of freedom, finally in the end turned every differend into a litigation).[43]

> Perhaps reflective responsibility today also consists in discerning, respecting, and making respected the differends, in establishing the incommensurability of the transcendental exigencies proper to heterogeneous phrase families, and to find other languages for what cannot be expressed within existing languages.[44]

One is probably faithful to Lyotard when suggesting that philosophy is the (non-hegemonic!) *discourse of the Idea of heterogeneity*. It is the task of the philosopher to foster this consciousness of heterogeneity – the consciousness that realizes at every event that this event is not to be grasped in language but that we cannot do anything else but precisely this. After all, there is always a phrase succeeding the linkage itself. Thus, philosophy ought to critique those who immediately try to fit the event into a hegemonic discourse; it cannot tolerate the easy reduction of differends to litigations and is compelled to bear witness to heterogeneity. Philosophy, therefore, can only pursue this task when it realizes that it is not a meta-language (D228). In other words, philosophy is a discourse genre that has as its rule *the constant search for its own rule* – its own presuppositions – with every investigation of other phrases, phrase regimens and discourse genres . . . (D98). Philosophical discourse ought to link phrases to each other such that it demonstrates that this linkage is not determined, but that the rule for the linkage must still be found (D180). Or, as Lyotard states in *Tombeau de l'intellectuel et autres papiers*:

> Philosophy is a discourse that has as its rule the search for its rule (and that of other discourses), a discourse in which phrases thus try themselves out without rules and link themselves guided only by amazement at the fact that everything has not been said, that a new phrase occurs, that it is not the case that nothing happens.[45]

Not forgetting the differend, then, implies regulating linkings in such a way that the differend itself is referred to in the linked phrase – whereby it is made clear that only one phrase could follow, even if many other phrases were indeed candidates. The second phrase in fact never succeeds in signifying the relative nothingness, the indeterminacy, the rule-lessness or the heterogeneity that separates the first phrase from the second. Moreover, we can describe the other side of the relative nothingness as a *radical otherness* which cannot be grasped or enclosed within a linked phrase. Bearing witness to the differend, then, is ultimately to bear witness to the heterogeneity that accompanies every linkage. In other words, the inexpressible (inconceivable, non-presentable) accompanies speech (conceiving, presenting), and even invites us to speak, but is never to be identified with the resulting articulated word or phrase. There is plurality because no phrase can exhaustively bring into discussion the inexpressible that asks to be put into phrases. In attempting this, the linked phrases cause a certain injustice to take place. Bearing witness to the differend means formulating links in such a way that the inexpressibility of the inexpressible is referred to. That is why, as already mentioned, the experience of the differend is the sensing of the *impossible phrase*: the sensing of the impossibility of the phrase which would succeed in expressing the inexpressible – the phrase which would succeed in articulating the event.

3

How to do justice to the event: The aesthetics of the sublime

The influence of Lyotard's *aesthetic* considerations on his postmodern language pragmatics is undeniable. As a matter of fact, in *Le postmoderne expliqué aux enfants* Lyotard enumerates four forms of expression of thought in which the postmodern problem comes to the fore: philosophy, politics, (visual) art and literature.[1] Elsewhere, he also mentions music (D192). In what follows, we will look somewhat closer into the form of art. First of all we will do so because, for Lyotard, the aesthetic and the historico-political (dealt with in his language pragmatics) are structured analogously.

> Undoubtedly both belong to the process of thinking that Kant called reflective judgment, which implies the ability of the mind to synthesize data, be it sensuous or socio-historical, without recourse to a predetermined rule.[2]

Moreover, in Lyotard's opinion, this demonstrates at the same time that bearing witness to the differend is not a discovery of our so-called postmodern age.

> All the investigations of the scientific, literary, and artistic avant-gardes over the past century have headed in this direction, the discovery of the incommensurability of the phrase regimes amongst them.[3]

Even stronger, if we – according to Lyotard – do not once again take up that which deeply concerned the modern avant-garde, we are condemned

> to repeat, without any displacement, the West's 'modern neurosis' – its schizophrenia, paranoia, and so on, the source of the misfortunes we have known for two centuries.[4]

In order to get started, we will first investigate the inspiration Lyotard took from Kant (and Burke). Afterwards, we will devote some thoughts to Lyotard's presentation of the avant-garde and how the postmodern is related to it.[5]

The beautiful and the sublime

Lyotard deems the rediscovery and interpretation of Kant's aesthetics of the sublime as very appropriate in order to analyse modern and postmodern art.[6] The aesthetics of Kant is contained in the first part of the *Kritik der Urteilskraft* (1790) in which Kant – after having dealt before with thinking and knowledge, will and action – critically examines feeling and imagination, paying attention to the relationships and transitions (passages) between the different faculties of thinking. The aesthetic experience is expressly situated within such a transition. In this regard, Kant distinguishes between an aesthetics of the beautiful and that of the sublime.

First, there is the aesthetics of *the beautiful*: an artwork, or an object from nature, can offer the person a feeling of pleasure, as a disinterested enjoyment, that arises in a harmonious conjunction of concept and image between the faculty of understanding and the free faculty of imagination (the faculty of sensibility). For Kant, this faculty of imagination offers us the capacity for presentation. On the one hand, it can be led by the intellect ('Verstand') – and thus, in Lyotard's vocabulary, functions in the verification-procedure of cognitive phrases by presenting the referent of these phrases. On the other hand, this faculty is also able to work in freedom: the free faculty of imagination is able to evoke images, those likewise 'imagined' or 'created' images. A feeling of beauty subsequently arises when an indeterminate concept originating in the intellect (and not a concrete concept, as then it would not be about the free faculty of imagination) is added to an image received in sensibility; in other words, when in seeing a work of art,

> given first by the sensibility and with no conceptual determination [the free faculty of imagination], arouses a feeling of pleasure that is independent of any interest [a disinterested enjoyment] and appeals to a principle of universal consensus (which may never be realized) [an indeterminate concept].[7]

The indeterminate harmony between intellect and imagination, between nature and image (i.e. nature contained in beautiful forms), provides a subjective feeling of pleasure that is nonetheless universally communicable, considering that the conditions for the experience of beauty anchored in the subject are a priori given in every subject. A beautiful entirety of sensible matter in an appropriate form is generally therefore enjoyed as a pleasurable thing.

This harmonious peace of the beautiful stands opposite to the turmoil of *the sublime*. The sublime is indeed as violent as a bolt of lightening and 'short-circuits thinking with itself'.[8] Very huge or powerful objects, like a mountain range and a pyramid or a storm and a volcanic eruption, can evoke the Idea of an absolute and boundless (a concept to which no images comply) 'matter' given to the sensibility for which no forms can be found. This inability-to-imagine brings about a particular suffering as a breach in the subject, or as a gap between what can be conceived of and what can be imagined. Harmony, intrinsic to the beautiful, is impossible here: the imagination undergoes a catastrophe, a disaster – the transition between the faculty of imagination and reason ('Vernunft') is experienced as being the utmost problematic. From this pain, however, arises a double satisfaction, a twofold feeling of pleasure. On the one hand, although a presentation of the Idea necessarily fails, the faculty of imagination attempts to present the un-presentable. On the other hand, the incapacity to imagine betrays the enormous power and superiority of the Ideas as well. This combined pleasure and pain, and the tension intrinsic to this combination, is specific for producing the feeling of the sublime.

> At the edge of the break, infinity, or the absoluteness of the Idea can be revealed in what Kant calls a negative presentation, or even a non-presentation.[9]

In other words, the faculty of the imagination does not succeed in ordering the data delivered by the senses into a fitting form, and precisely in this incapacity an Idea of reason, something absolute in size or in power, is made 'quasi perceptible'.[10] For Kant, this absolute is the Idea of freedom. The aesthetics of the sublime is a passageway for revealing the lofty calling of the person to freedom. For that purpose, the aesthetics of the beautiful is given up and broken. Within this connection, Lyotard speaks of the aesthetic experience of the sublime 'as a sign of transcendence in the ethical' and likewise of the 'sacrificial proclamation of ethics in the aesthetic'.[11] The feeling of the sublime, given in the tension of discomfort and double pleasure, reveals to the person his or her being-spirit, as well as their ultimate spiritual destiny. Nature in its formlessness – the incapacity of the sensibility to find forms for the offered matter – lets true being-human shine precisely through the breach of the faculty of imagination and thus signifies its own sacrifice, its own 'disappearance'.

Lyotard borrows this feeling of the sublime from Kant in order to describe the feeling of the event, of the 'it is happening'. The feeling of the sublime reveals the differend between the phrases and discourse genres. In a unity that is impossible to present, the sublime brings before us both the absolutely infinite and the absolutely finite, and thus bears witness to the incommensurability between reason and imagination.

Lyotard links his reading of Kant's conceptualization of the aesthetics of the sublime, as the combination of discomfort-pleasure in relation to the attempt to present something that does not let itself be presented, with elements from the aesthetic theory of Edmund Burke.[12] For the latter, the sublime is affixed to the threat that nothing happens anymore, the threat of 'is it (still) happening?'. The absolute summoned in the experience of huge or powerful situations leads to 'terror', an anxiety caused by being deprived of light, the other, language, things, life: the anxiety that 'it is happening' no longer happens. The suspension of this anxiety by taking away the threat, then produces a feeling of pleasure, an enlightenment of sorts: 'delight' itself. The feeling of the sublime, however, rests in the combination of both (suspended) anxiety and pleasure (on account of the suspension).[13] Or, put differently, the feeling of the sublime is not an uplifting feeling but one of intensification.

The avant-garde and postmodern aesthetics

According to Lyotard, the *modern avant-garde* took an aesthetics of the sublime as its starting point:

> Showing that there is something we can conceive of which we can neither see nor show.[14]

Visible presentations, often abstract, formless, and deviating from the 'usual', are intended to refer to what could not be presented directly, evoking a sense of interruption and ungraspability. Everything that served the purposes of representation became questionable: the figurative, colour, lines, frame, exposition hall, etc. The avant-garde inquired into the conditions of space and time, the *conditions of the presentation*. It was not the subject of artwork that was important, but the 'it is happening', or better, the 'is it happening?', to which the work intended to bear witness.[15] The experience evoked among spectators as a consequence was neither a feeling of the beautiful, nor an ethical calling, but an intensification of their emotional and conceptual capacities: 'une jouissance ambivalente'.[16]

While painting, the painter consciously had in mind the goal of answering the question 'what is a painting?'. The avant-garde, by practising such methods, in fact attempted to answer the question about the implicit presuppositions of modernity.

Due to the fact that these artworks were not understood, they were generally not accepted and only later preserved and displayed in museums.[17] Unlike the aesthetics of the beautiful, the turmoil of the aesthetics of the sublime could not appeal to a sense of universal communicability, to a shared disinterested enjoyment. Rather, the ungraspability of the avant-garde and the fierce emotions that it could arouse were labelled as dangerous (to the state) and were countered by specific attempts to neutralize the 'event' in repressive art-politics.[18] The avant-garde indeed revolutionized those symbolic images with which the community identified itself and, as such, destabilized the status quo.

It is precisely the *radicalization of this programme of the modern avant-garde* that comprises the essence of postmodern art. For the modern avant-garde presented the unpresentable still within a nostalgic longing for a vanished beginning or end, a foundational or anticipated presence no longer available. That which was recognizable in this longing continued to offer some comfort and joy. Postmodern aesthetics, however, no longer knows this nostalgia and is only aware of the impossible presentation of the unpresentable. It is

> that which . . . invokes the unpresentable in presentation itself, that which refuses the consolation of correct forms, refuses the consensus of taste permitting a common experience of nostalgia for the impossible, and inquires into new presentations – not to take pleasure in them, but to better produce the feeling that there is something unpresentable.[19]

> Today's 'modernity' does not expect the *aisthesis* to give the soul the peace of lovely consent, but precisely that it snatch it out of nothingness.[20]

Such aesthetic experience, whose intensity depends on the extent of the variability, fluidity, agitation and evanescence of what is being presented, stands as the model for the attitude in which the postmodern person is active in the world. Just as one cannot grasp a flame and cannot affix the contours of a flowing stream (as examples taken from Kant), the postmodern person wants to let events happen as they do. This means taking a distance from those attempts at recuperating or confining the now-moment or the event; this means restraining from making history by inscribing everything into one narrative. It is letting the now-moment interrupt, and being taken by surprise. Such an interruptive event is not the product of human consciousness, but precedes it (and is always to be forgotten when stabilizing one's identity). Receptivity, 'passibilité', contemplativity, presupposes indeed a gift that is not yet mediated by 'concepts'.

His analysis of the aesthetic of the sublime has taught Lyotard that precisely the tension between the impossibility of expressing the unpresentable in phrases, colours, sounds, and pictures, and the feeling one experiences that this nevertheless must be done, is essential for a postmodern aesthetic. In this regard, the *sublime sensing of the non-presentable is structurally analogous to the sublime sensing of heterogeneity* – the sign of history on behalf of postmodern times. The 'now-moment' that the painter wants to entrust to the canvas is analogous to the event to which the linked phrase intends to bear witness.[21] Philosophy, literature, music, and the plastic arts, which received their form in institutions, schools, programmes, and traditions, should therefore be broken open and disarmed. As in language pragmatics – where philosophy is looking for the impossible phrase, and attempting to present the interruptive event of the differend in the linking of phrases in the unfolding of a discourse – contemporary aesthetics pays tribute to the unpresentable, which lies at the core of all (re)presentation.

4

Postmodern critical theory in action: The case of capitalism

It has been critically remarked that Lyotard's views would lead to a radical relativism which, if understood as the super-structure of late capitalism, would display conservative characteristics. Jürgen Habermas, for example, labelled Lyotard as an adept young-conservative, a criticism he also made of other postmodern thinkers of difference such as Jacques Derrida.[1] For such young-conservatives, the crisis of modernity consists in the link between modernity and rationality. The rejection of this link brings them, according to Habermas, to a kind of anti-modernism, which – paradoxically! – starts off from the aesthetics of modernity (the discovery of a decentred subjectivity). The antidotes the young-conservatives apply against instrumental reason, by this count, are the spontaneous forces of the imaginary which can only be called upon evocatively (articulated in the will-to-power, the Dionysian power – a terminology in which Nietzsche's influence is not unfamiliar). What remains is anarchistic multiplicity.

As far as Richard Rorty is concerned, Lyotard falsely assumes that his 'ironic philosophy' of the private intellectual would also work in terms of social objectives. Lyotard's plea for dissensus is perhaps interesting for his personal endeavours, Rorty concedes, but as concerns the political, the establishment of consensus is of capital importance. Rendered in terms of the aesthetic categories of the 'beautiful' and the 'sublime', Rorty concludes:

> Social purposes are served, just as Habermas says, by finding beautiful ways of harmonising interests, rather than sublime ways of detaching oneself from others' interests. The attempt of leftist intellectuals [like Lyotard] to pretend that the avant-garde is serving the wretched of the earth by fighting free of the merely beautiful is a hopeless attempt to make the special needs of the intellectual and the social needs of her community coincide.[2]

In order to deal with this criticism, we will consider in this chapter Lyotard's criticism of capitalism. It will become clear that in his plea to bear witness to the differend, Lyotard unfolds a critical potential that is not a side effect of his philosophy, but belongs to its core. We will introduce Lyotard's critical theory of postmodern capitalism both from his aesthetic and language pragmatic philosophy. We will accordingly first discuss the capitalist sublation of the avant-garde and then unfold the alliance between capitalism and the techno-scientific complex. Afterwards, we will further explain Lyotard's postmodern critical theory as he developed this throughout his many publications.

The capitalist rejection of the avant-garde

The (post)modern aesthetic sensibility has raised many critical remarks. In many of these, however, Lyotard discerns a longing for order, unity, identity, safety and popularity – solid ground on which to stand. Habermas, for example, according to Lyotard, changes the status of the aesthetic experience in such a way that aesthetics can be deemed competent to bridge the heterogeneity between the cognitive, ethical and political discourses.[3] Whatever or whoever goes against this desire for unity, against such new realism, is criticized, and one is eager to *forget about the legacy of the avant-garde*. While the art-politics of Nazi Germany and Stalinist Russia exposed an anti-modern striving for realism (by structuring the aesthetic judgement analogous to the cognitive judgement), today – Lyotard complains – attempts are made to outshine the avant-garde in a trans-avant-gardism or in a (uncritical) postmodernism like that of Charles Jencks.[4] These attempts are characterized by an eclecticism: everything is deemed possible and ultimately results in kitsch. The avant-garde is not banished, as in repressive Nazi-politics, but uprooted and delivered to the capitalist culture-industry. In the current society ruled by the law of capital, the lack of aesthetic standards has led to a situation in which the value of an art work can be expressed only in purely financial terms. There is also in this case, a striving towards realism: a 'realism of Anything Goes' which is 'the realism of money'.[5] In both cases, it concerns a realism, which can be defined only by its intention of avoiding the question of reality implied in the question of art.[6]

Vulgar postmodern art is marked by mass conformism: one sells to the public only that which it already likes.[7] Such art is about the satisfaction of longings, a furnishing with uniformity, simplicity, communicability, recognition and stability. This 'uncritical' postmodernism deprives the artist of his or her responsibility to bear witness to the unpresentable, and it suits those artists who are not willing to accept responsibility. It produces 'culture' in the service of the status quo and operates according to the economic laws of the market.

Put more subtly, the capitalist rejection of the avant-garde consists in the ambiguous, even perverse alliance between present economic premises – the creation of new markets, of demand – and a *corrupted aesthetics of the sublime*. To achieve artistic as well as commercial success, one has to work as follows, according to Lyotard:

> One re-uses formulae confirmed by previous success, one throws them off-balance by combining them with other, in principle incompatible, formulae, by amalgamations, quotations, ornamentations, pastiche. One can go as far as kitsch or the grotesque. One flatters the 'taste' of a public that can have no taste, and the eclecticism or a sensibility enfeebled by the multiplication of available forms and objects. In this way one thinks that one is expressing the spirit of the times, whereas one

is merely reflecting the spirit of the market. Sublimity is no longer in art, but in speculation on art.[8]

The contemporary aesthetic sensitivity for experiences of interruption then is called upon to conceal the fact that, in a hegemonic economizing discourse, nothing really 'happens' any more. The economizing discourse 'processes' current aesthetic tendencies in order to revitalize and reaffirm itself. This has of course serious consequences for the aesthetic realm. The joint activity of economy and aesthetics only takes place at a superficial level, and leads in fact to the mere insertion of the aesthetic discourse into the totalizing, economizing narrative. As a result, the aesthetic sensitivity for interruptive experiences is subtly, and also radically, damaged, and the event character of the experience of the sublime is ruled out. Art is bought and sold as pseudo-event, functioning within, and not interruptive to, the ongoing economic discourse. Art no longer reflects the critical consciousness of our time, but becomes an image of the market. The plea of so-called postmodern aesthetic theories for a free-wheeling artistic playfulness, is in reality co-opted by this alliance of the aesthetic and the market, and promoted by a silent, all-encompassing economic master narrative.

Language pragmatic analysis of capitalism

When examining capitalism from a language pragmatic perspective, Lyotard explains that modern (and contemporary) capitalism is the *merger of four genres of discourse* – that is, four discourses of an Idea: a kind of coalition or alliance of the political, scientific, and technological discourses with the economic discourse.[9] The latter is ruled by the Idea of profit; political discourse strives for the common good;[10] the discourse of science is guided by the Idea of perfect knowledge; and technological discourse attempts to reach the highest degree of performance and efficiency. In capitalism, these four discourses are related to one another. First of all, there is an alliance of the economic and the political discourses resulting in a mixed economy: states participate in the economic discourse, for example as banker, employer and employee. Second, technological and scientific discourses also enter into an alliance with each other, and, by doing so, thoroughly change the nature of knowledge: the technological discourse provides criteria to validate cognitive claims, and scientific research is most often carried out in view of its possible applications. Capitalism then is finally the merger between both alliances: the techno-scientific alliance is co-opted by the alliance between capital and state, which, for example, has resulted in big industries associated with the military, space travel, nuclear energy and others – recently also the eco-industry. In what follows, we will discuss both alliances and indicate how the techno-scientific alliance drives capitalism to its ultimate limits. We will conclude by showing what the impact is hereof for 'culture' and its capacity to recognize differends.

As Lyotard writes in Le différend, until recently, *capitalism*, as the hegemony of the economic genre, was often considered a modern universal narrative, closely linked to the modern narratives of emancipation, and promising humanity a better future by the spreading of welfare. This, however, only served as a legitimating arrangement because in the hegemonic economic discourse, the political question on the public good is actually not raised, not even when the political discourse itself is involved in economics (D253). In the end, the economic narrative only goes about the accumulation of capital, of money, and therefore concerns the gain of time – Lyotard speaks here of dominating time through money.[11] The rules for linking phrases in the economic genre are clear – and show the domination of time through money: when phrase 'x' [addressor 'a' hands over referent 'c' to addressee 'b'] is the case, then phrase 'y' ['b' gives referent 'd' to 'a'] is presupposed. The linkage is thus not only expected, but even presupposed from the outset: what is programmed is exchange. Phrase 'x' makes 'b' into one who stands in debt to 'a'; phrase 'y' cancels this debt (D240–41). While the narrative attempts to acknowledge the event (the debt) and maintain it (reductively) by encapsulating it within the larger whole, phrase 'y' immediately attempts to erase, or to undo the event (causing debt) of phrase 'x' in the hegemonic discourse (D254). Capitalism therefore establishes an all-encompassing market situation of exchange (D255), where 'nothing really happens' anymore, because events (time) are calculated and predicted, thus radically weakened in their capacity as interruptive now-moments. The expectation of the phrase to come, as the event, is 'erased' by the coercive logic of 'exchange' (D260). Everything is reduced to time, to the 'indifference of money'.[12]

Already in *La condition postmoderne*, Lyotard investigated the *alliance of science and technology*, wherein he especially emphasized the encapsulation of the question of truth in the demand for performativity. The technologies that resulted from this, and especially the 'computerization' of our world, have brought about a qualitative transformation of knowledge.[13] To begin with, computer technology detemporalizes (and delocalizes) the knowledge written down in culture's memory (which is as a synthesis of time). Elements of knowledge, always acquired in a particular 'here and now', are 'scanned' and become digitalized as they are converted into data, which subsequently function independently of addressor, addressee, original space and time. These elements are extracted from their original synthesis, their traditions and local cultures, and can as such be taken up in new syntheses. Knowledge becomes universally readable, available, useful, usable and operational. This not only means that the function of memory (and thus the saving of time) changes, but also that the reflexive relationship with regard to the past – and the knowledge and creative possibilities contained there for the present, are thoroughly displaced as well. The bounds of traditions disappear in a techno-scientific 'scanning' of knowledge. Data can be combined in an unlimited way, and new syntheses and 'surprising' discoveries can be made as well, though background knowledge and broader frameworks disappear, creating a reality that makes Lyotard conclude:

More knowledge and power, yes – but why, no.[14]

Moreover, the stringent demand for the perfection of performance enforces this never-ending process of 'scanning' and combining data. A techno-scientific discourse aims at recording all possible combinations in its formalized memory. All possible 'events' are thereby eliminated, because what can be known and predicted no longer 'happens' or really surprises. This results not only in an anticipation of the future, but also – and more so – in a *recuperation of the future*:

Better: what comes 'after' the 'now' will have to come 'before' it.[15]

A techno-scientific discourse thus predicts the event and dominates time. Taking this into account, it is not difficult to understand the encompassing alliance between capitalism and techno-scientific discourse since both are about the mastery of time. Scientific research, especially with its high-technological conditioning of procedures of verification/falsification, demands large sums of money. Capital, as saved time, is invested in order to move forward in time. In this way, economic discourse, along with its techno-scientific ally, recuperates the event by anticipating it.

In the end, all domains of human life and their specific discourses become reductively integrated into one hegemonic narrative, ruled by, and obedient to, the market law of supply and demand. Culture thereby becomes entirely commodified. The hegemony of the alliance between techno-scientific, (corrupted) aesthetic, and (political-)economic discourses transforms culture into a culture-industry. The event-character of the 'will-it-happen?' is stripped of its possible unpredictable, surprising, creative and unexpected character. Furthermore, elements of other discourses and narratives are extracted from their spatio-temporal settings and fragmented into single entities. Cultural legacies are broken up into free 'bits', which can then be combined in an unlimited way. Through this, again, possible events are strategically anticipated and thus become pseudo-events, 'pseudo-now-moments', manufactured forms of intensity. As mentioned, degenerated postmodern art functions in this way; its perversity lies in the production and sale of (pseudo-)events. 'Time' becomes mere availability, marketability, consumability or manageability. Fashionable words – like difference, alterity, singularity, subculture, subaltern – are streamlined by this culture-industry as commodified references to the unpresentable in the (cultural) market. From this perspective, aestheticization comes to mean little more than 'spectacle', and this in a twofold respect: as created (and thus pseudo-) events and as concerns its visibility/ tangibility. This results in:

A human community who contemplates its differences [. . . ;] a humanity viewing the spectacle of itself in every theater.[16]

Everything appears to be foreign, but nothing really is.

Postmodern critical theory

From this analysis, the critical potential of Lyotard's theory of postmodernity becomes clear. The hegemony of the economic master narrative cannot boast any legitimacy, since this genre of discourse is only one among many others. With the help of his language pragmatic vocabulary Lyotard is able to detect the insidious, and not immediately observable, danger of this domination. As a hegemonic discourse, the economic genre, in fact, not only regulates the linkages, but – even more so – anticipates and recuperates their event-character. Moreover, it offers the semblance of taking these events seriously, while in actuality producing them.

In contrast to such a series of deceptions, Lyotard sets before us the task of bearing witness to the differend, and, as such, he calls for thinkers, painters, authors, and musicians to engage the conflicting heterogeneity involved in a situation of plurality, specifically so as to unmask all pretensions of hegemony. To avoid all confusion, he refers to postmodernity as a matter of *rewriting modernity* ('Durcharbeitung').[17] Such rewriting, however, concerns not simply an investigation of the past, in order to thoroughly examine the whole of modernity again and pass an independent judgement on it. Nor does it imply that the mistakes of modernity are reviewed and corrected, thus fulfilling the destiny of modernity. After all, the history of the fate of modernity would then be encapsulated once again within a hegemonic narrative, predictably at the cost of our own deception. The rewriting of modernity Lyotard seeks can only be an endeavour without a regulating goal. It demands receptivity, and a readiness not to judge too hastily, analogous to current (uncorrupted) postmodern aesthetic sensibilities. The past in this view is not *re*presented as such, but presents itself, not as knowledge about the past, but in forms that are newly discovered. Rewriting consequently boils down to a remembering of what one actually should not/cannot forget because it never was or can be written down: it is an already shattered presence of which only the interruptive event can be remembered, and which in itself can never be grasped.[18]

Some years later, however, in *Moralités postmodernes*, Lyotard warned of the pitfall awaiting even his own critique of capitalism. He had become very conscious, he then ascertained, that his work now functioned differently within society than it did a few years previously. Where critique then used to be considered as taking an offensive stance with regard to the system and as invariably ending in social rejection, it had now become an internally *calculated reflex of systemic auto-correction*. Instead of being troubled by the alternative and its critique, the present system not only allowed for diversity, but even welcomed critique. The system created a large margin of uncertainty, of open space where discussion, deviation and dissent are possible. At the same time, however, it also set the rules regarding non-consent: an underlying consensus precedes all dissent. Every critical contribution was finally evaluated in light of the system's own perceived perfection; critique is thus systemically streamlined and regulated by its fundamental principle of exchangeability. The keywords therefore became: dialogue, conversation, interaction, communication.[19] However, Lyotard protested, just as not being allowed to speak – an imposed silence – should be labelled as a form of terror, so too should enforced speech and banished silence. Thinking, painting, writing and composing, should never be preceded by consensus. Real critique must always strive to be system-transcendent, and refuse to merely fill up the blank spaces left open by the system. Only allowing for a pure system-immanent critique ends in totalitarianism, since it attempts to exclude in advance what cannot be systematically integrated.[20]

Diversity, heterogeneity, singularity, pluricentrism, the collapse of rationality and meaning into fragments, a sundry of traces, each of these offer no guarantees for a well-understood concept of postmodernity. All of them are at risk of functioning as market strategies. Time and again, the heterogeneity of the event, the other in the self, risks being forgotten. Perhaps for this reason, and due to the many concealed attempts at totalization he perceived to be everywhere, Lyotard again named in *Moralités postmodernes* the unnamed feeling of our time: *melancholy*.[21]

By way of conclusion: Lyotard's intuition expressed in a plurality of perspectives

After *La condition postmoderne* in 1979, Lyotard deepened and nuanced his theory of postmodernity.[22] He revised and expanded his language pragmatic framework, previously restricted to narrativity and scientific discursiveness, to include all possible language expressions. This move was accompanied by a more critical view on the techno-scientific discourse and the demand for performativity, especially because of the all-too-easy alliance between techno-scientific and hegemonic economic discourses. The status of paralogy, understood in *La condition postmoderne* as the deviant small narrative that helps science in its development, is thus set within a broader framework, and Lyotard continually warns against the lurking danger of pseudo-paralogy. Finally, there is a sharper development of the link between knowledge and politics. In *Le différend*, for example, politics is described as the field where the genres of discourse wrestle with each other in order to be able to link onto the preceding phrase. Philosophy, therefore, has direct political implications. It is called to operate as a reflexive faculty of judgement that analyses the political field, establishes heterogeneity between the families of phrases, studies the transitions between the phrases and makes one respect the differends; it is a genre that knows that it must always still find its own rule.

Lyotard's interest in aesthetics offers him, moreover, the opportunity to interpret the processes of postmodern aestheticization in light of an aesthetics of the sublime, with a special attentiveness for openness and receptivity. Postmodern culture – as the work of the painter, sculptor, author, musician and philosopher – develops a sensibility for the differend to which one must bear witness; a feeling that at the same time allows the hegemony of performativity and capital to be put under critique; a feeling that cannot permit the role of authority to be occupied by a particular instance, since this leads to terror; a feeling, finally, that remains however *without a demonstrable normative instance*. Indeed, the answer to the question where the command to offer resistance obtains its legitimacy from, must remain open, Lyotard claims.

> It is to be thought that this order orders that the question be left open, if it is true that this 'you must' preserves and reserves the coming of the future in its unexpectedness.[23]

Lyotard's postmodern critical theory ultimately intends to bear witness to the differend – the event to be appreciated not because of its newness but because of its shattering, interrupting character – that is, not for the 'what' but for the 'that' of the event. In a postmodern context there is no longer a need for master narratives, but for 'micrologies' that accompany metaphysics in its fall. As Lyotard adds in reference to Adorno:

> Micrology inscribes the occurrence of a thought as the unthought that remains to be thought in the decline of 'great' philosophical thought.[24]

During his career, and in many different ways and modes, Lyotard himself had taken to heart this task to bear witness to the differend. He was well aware that it is no easy task, without efforts, without doubts, without pain. Bearing witness to the 'other' inhuman (the ungraspable inhuman within the human, the indeterminate of childhood), he offered resistance to the inhuman encapsulation of humanity: differentiation turning into indifferentism, a negative entropy controlled by the capitalist techno-scientific complex.

> Human beings taken away by an inhuman development, which one no longer dares to call progress. The disappearance of a human, political and philosophical alternative to such a process. Only a resistance based on another inhuman is still possible: the dispossession of oneself, which sleeps in each human being, one's indomitable infancy.[25]

In many other publications as well he engaged in this work in similar ways. In *Lectures d'enfance*, for instance, he discusses the work of Kafka, Sartre, Joyce, Freud, Valéry and Arendt, and finds in their writings what he has called the unpresentable within an aesthetic perspective, something expressed differently time and again:

> Kafka calls this the indubitable, Sartre the inarticulable, Joyce the inappropriable. For Freud, it is the infantile, for Valéry disorder, for Arendt birth.[26]

Lyotard himself speaks about *infantia*,

> that which does not speak for itself. An infancy which is not an age of life and which does not pass. It haunts the discourse. It continues to split the latter, it is its separation. However, precisely at that point [the discourse] keeps on constituting it,

as lost. Without knowing, it offers it shelter. It is its rest. If the
infancy stays with [the discourse], it is not despite it, but because
it is staying with the adult.[27]

Perhaps we can learn from Jewish thought, he states elsewhere, not
to ask for an answer, but to ask in order to remain in the question
itself. For the Jewish tradition, all reality is a dark message of an
unknown, unnamed addressor.[28]

*   *   *

If perhaps there is something to learn from Jewish thought on this
matter, then, we might ask, is there also something to be learned
from Christian thought? In many ways, it would seem not.

5

The master narrative of Christianity: A hegemonic discourse of the Idea of love

When Lyotard, in *Le postmoderne expliqué aux enfants*, distinguished between master narratives, the first one he mentioned was the Christian narrative of the 'redemption of original sin through love',[1] and only afterwards the speculative master narrative of knowledge and the master narratives of emancipation brought about during the Enlightenment, in Marxism and in modern capitalism. As we have seen, from the perspective of Lyotard's language pragmatics, the main problem of master narratives is diagnosed as a severe and structural forgetfulness of the differend, which results in massive forms of injustice. The totalizing way in which a master narrative arranges the linkage of phrases does not allow for otherness to halt – even momentarily – the steady and uninterrupted progression of the narrative. In this chapter we will present and further elaborate on Lyotard's critical analysis of the Christian master narrative. We will take up again the four characteristics of master narratives we distinguished with Lyotard, and will attempt to show on the basis of indications from Lyotard, but also adding our own examples and considerations, how the Christian narrative can indeed be analysed as a master narrative, and, more precisely, as the hegemonic discourse of the Idea of love. Afterwards, in the following chapter, we will further inquire whether (the Christian) God can escape the clutches of the Christian master narrative, and provide answers as to where a theologian's conversation with Lyotard might lead.

In *Le différend*, Lyotard speaks about the master narrative of Christianity in only four statements (D232–35), and elsewhere it would seem that there are only occasional references to Christianity.[2] However, in *Le différend*, Lyotard portrays the Christian narrative as the master narrative par excellence, mainly because of its ability to realize, in an extremely efficient way, the goal of the narrative genre.

> [B]etween two narratives belonging to the same genre, one can be judged stronger than the other if it comes nearer to the goal of narratives: to link onto the occurrence as such by signifying it and referring to it. The Christian narrative vanquished the other narratives in Rome because by introducing the love of occurrence into narratives and narrations of narratives, it designated what is at stake in the genre itself. To love what happens as if it were a gift, to love even the *Is it happening?* as the promise of good news, allows for linking onto whatever happens, including other narratives (and, subsequently, even other genres).[3]

Because of its introduction of love for the event, Christianity became a very powerful master narrative: because it is loved, the event itself, along with all its possible newness and otherness, is always already narratively recuperated from within the Christian narrative.

As already mentioned, in the end, for Lyotard, a modern master narrative can be unmasked as a *hegemonic discourse of the Idea*, which largely explains the distinction made with regard to pre-modern myths. For Christianity this then would be the Idea of love. Taken in its own right, an Idea is a general, universal principle that refers to a quasi-referent – in other words, something to which the referent cannot be directly presented, or can only be indirectly presented through symbols or signs. In a modern master narrative, however, this particular nature of the Idea is forgotten, for within such a discourse, (a) the Idea is the goal that legitimizes the narrative from the end, (b) it universalizes the instances of the universe of phrases, (c) it explains reality (and thus its referent can be presented), and (d) it regulates the linking of the phrases in an exclusive and thus hegemonic way (e.g. connecting prescriptive phrases to descriptive ones quasi-automatically), while at the same time discrediting whoever links (= thinks or talks) differently.

In the following we will elaborate on Lyotard's evaluation of Christianity by way of these four characteristics to determine its hegemonic narrative nature, including the role of the Idea of love.

Legitimation from the end

First of all, modern master narratives no longer consist of a set of many small narratives that legitimize culture from its beginnings (e.g. by telling of an original founding act, or explaining why things have become what they are), but they constitute all-encompassing narratives of history which legitimize themselves from the end, goal or finality of history.

Here it would seem that Christianity does not as such answer to this characteristic, and that the Christian narrative is not legitimized proceeding from the end. Rather Christianity stems from a *particular, partly mythical, narrative tradition.* The roots of the Christian narrative lie in a canonized set of stories, so that one comes to conclude that its legitimation comes from the origin, or its beginnings, rather than from the end, or its sense of finality. An exegetical investigation regarding the more ancient narrative traditions of the Old Testament can provide further explanation on this matter. It is probable that a collection of small narratives on the God of Abraham, Isaac, Jacob, Joseph, Moses and many others, functioned in the same way as the collection of narratives among the Cashinahua Indians, namely, as a universe of names that accorded to the individual his or her identity. Creation and fall narratives (Gen. 2–3), as well as exodus and covenant ones, retell the founding deeds. Through narration and ritual, these deeds are reappropriated and identity is received from such acts. Precisely during the Paschal celebration, when children invite their father to narrate the origins of the Pascha, they all participate together, by word and gesture, in this foundational event. Everyone present is socialized into the narrative and lives within its space.

Yet the Jewish religion did not remain a religious narrative that was exclusively determined from the past. On the contrary, a historical dynamism unfolded wherein the future acquired an increasingly more significant place. There arose expectations and hopes for life in the 'Promised Land', for the coming of the Messiah, for the definitive salvation of the Jewish people and, later, in a more universal dimension, of all other peoples as well. Origin and end are hereby involved together.

Jesus of Nazareth lies at the origin of a re-narration and a return to the sources, a recontextualization of these narratives. In the literature that has come to be written about him and his message, it is difficult to determine how far he himself preached this future-oriented and universal dimension. It is equally difficult to determine in the writings of the first Christian authors whether it is the origin or the end that serves to legitimize. Does the resurrection-event need to be understood as a promise or as an anticipation of the resurrection of everyone at the end of time, or should it rather be understood as a foundational deed to which Christians participate in word and gesture, in story and ritual? Perhaps origin and end also come together here.

From the perspective of Lyotard's argument, special attention should be given to the more reflexive discourse which appears in the gospels and the epistles, in contrast to the more narrative character of the largest parts of the Bible. In this discourse, an important place is set aside for 'love'.[4] Love fulfils the entire law (Rom. 13,10b). Love is present at the beginning and at the end. Christians ought to love one another, just as and because God, in Jesus Christ, first loved them (Jn 13,34). This causes Lyotard to conclude that the Idea of love determines the Christian hegemonic narrative. Nevertheless, however, in *Le differend*, Lyotard suggests that its legitimation proceeds from the beginning and not from the end. He considers revelation as a narrative both about and from the authorizing origin:

The narrative of authorization in its beginnings, which determines its ends.[5]

Christianity, from his perspective, is therefore foremost a universal narrative established 'as progress towards the salvation of all creatures' because it is grounded in the revelation of an authoritative primordial story. In contradistinction to the Christian narrative, 'humanity' in modern narratives

is not made of creatures in the process of redeeming themselves, but of wills in the process of emancipating themselves.

Authorization does not reside in a myth of beginnings, but in an Idea which exerts its finality upon phrases and which ought to allow for a way to regulate the differends between genres.[6]

Also in *Le postmoderne expliqué aux enfants*, he speaks expressly about the Christian narrative of the restoration of Adam's fault.

Therefore the hegemonic narrative of Christianity cannot as such be called 'modern', if 'modern' here would mean an exclusive orientation towards the future, as towards the realization of the Idea. However, perhaps it is more appropriate to state that Christianity *combines the legitimation from both origin and end* – although it is clear that before modernity, legitimation proceeding from the origin received more weight, and probably progressively a shift took place towards a legitimation proceeding from the end. In other places, and explicitly in *Moralités postmodernes*, Lyotard seems to go along with this view when he indicates that the first traces of modernity are to be found in the work of Paul of Tarsus and Augustine. They in fact usher in the notion of historicity, so essential for modernity, by conceiving of a Christian eschatology oriented towards the completion of history.

> Eschatology recounts the experience of a subject affected by a lack, and prophesies that this experience will finish at the end of time with the remission of evil, the destruction of death, and the return to the Father's house, that is, to the full signifier.[7]

Christian hope then is the prototype for the modern expectation of the subject's reconciliation with itself at the end of history – a completion that Lyotard now affirms is the fulfilment of the promise of a lost perfect beginning:

> An immemorial past is always what turns out to be promised by way of an ultimate end . . . Eschatology calls for an archaeology.[8]

Once emancipated from the link to this particular Christian tradition, modern master narratives are exclusively legitimated by their finality, and love becomes transformed into republican brotherhood or communist solidarity (D235).

The universalization of the instances

Second, a modern master narrative has universal pretensions. For that purpose, it erases all particular names and keeps only general categories. The four instances of the phrase universe (addressor, addressee, referent and sense) are universalized.

Precisely as in Marxism, where the Idea of the emancipated proletariat universalizes the instances of the phrase universe, in the Christian master narrative it is the Idea of love that takes hold of them. God, who is love, as addressor tells us addressees the story about love (referent): 'because I, who am love, have loved you, you must love (me)'. We note here, as well, the circularity and displacement of the Idea over each of the four instances. Love reveals itself to those who open themselves in love to it.

> The authorization to tell, to listen, and to be told about does not result from a common affiliation with a world of names which are themselves descended from primordial narratives, it results from a commandment of universal attraction, *Love one another*, addressed to all heroes, all narrators, and all narratees. This commandment is authorized by the revelation (itself loving) of a primordial story in which we learn that the god of love was not very well loved by his children and about the misfortunes that ensued. This authorization remains in the circular form common to all narratives, but is extended to all narratives. The obligation to love is decreed by the divine Absolute, it is addressed to all creatures (who are none other than His addressees), and it becomes transitive (in an interested sense, because it is conditional): if you are loved, you ought to love; and you shall be loved only if you love.[9]

Texts from the New Testament could give Lyotard sufficient reason to think so. See for example Jn 14,21–23, and especially 1 Jn 4, 7–12:

> [7]Dear friends, let us love one another, for love comes from God. Everyone who loves has been born of God and knows God. [8]Whoever does not love does not know God, because God is love. [9]This is how God showed his love among us: He sent his one and only Son into the world that we might live through him.

> [10]This is love: not that we loved God, but that he loved us and sent his Son as an atoning sacrifice for our sins. [11]Dear friends, since God so loved us, we also ought to love one another. [12]No one has ever seen God; but if we love one another, God lives in us and his love is made complete in us. (1 Jn 4,7–12)

The universalizing of the instances entails the transformation of the particular instances in local stories and the undoing of their particularity. Because of this, the local narratives themselves change: they are inscribed within the master narrative and start to function with reference to the Idea of love.

> Thanks to the precepts of love, all of the events already told in the narrative of infidels and unbelievers can be re-told as so many signs portentous of the new commandment.[10]

> Love supplied with its narrative of authorization can engender a universal history as progress towards the redemption of creatures.[11]

Cognitive pretension

Third, like myths, master narratives think that they can describe reality truthfully, thus betraying a cognitive pretension: they claim to present reality as it is.

Insofar as the Christian narrative assumes love as the dynamic force that drives history towards its completion, it claims thereby to describe reality according to truth. The Christian master narrative holds to a *cognitive claim*: love is what reality is about, and it offers us a reading key to approach and evaluate whatever 'happens'. Once this is accepted, the distinction between history and the history of salvation is no longer of any help, but must itself be acknowledged as a consequence of the power of the hegemonic narrative to describe reality: salvation history is the result of what the dynamism of love historically actualizes, and history then is the field (neutral or otherwise) in which this dynamism establishes salvation history. The hegemonic narrative as such offers a gauge with which to judge historical events. Insomuch as they contribute to a sense of completion in love, they are ascribed to the dynamic of love – the Holy Spirit, as it is called within the Christian narrative. If they do not contribute, they harm this dynamic and are designated as evil, sinful or even demonic. Therefore the narrative enables Christians to legitimately judge concerning what was, what is and what is to come.

This cognitive pretension becomes even more explicitly visible when the addressor-instance (by replacement) is taken in by an institution, a doctrinal authority, or a magisterium, that parades itself as the spokesperson of love and deems itself able to make authoritative pronouncements within a cognitive language concerning history and reality.

A hegemonic discourse

Finally, master narratives are known as closed hegemonic discourses that automatically regulate the linkages, thereby subordinating other discourse genres. As such, they have no difficulty in linking descriptive and prescriptive phrases to each other. They legitimate institutions, social and individual life, politics, ethics, legislation, etc. Moreover, due to the absence of legitimate external criticism, the hegemony of the narrative remains unquestioned.

As was already mentioned, the narrative genre of discourse easily forgets the multiplicity of diverse incommensurable phrase regimens and genres of discourse. A narrative quasi-automatically regulates the linkages and so reduces the event to a litigation – however, it does so not by negating the relative nothingness between two sentences, that is, by denying the event, but by retelling it, giving it a meaning, and recuperating it into the greater whole. The better a narrative succeeds in doing that, the greater the power of the narrative. Therefore, according to Lyotard, the Christian narrative, with its focus on the love for the event, is to be evaluated as very powerful, because it succeeds in making links with 'whatever happens' (D232). The event is not stashed away, but rather stripped of its interruptive otherness by being immediately registered in the Christian narrative as a gracious gift of love, that is, as grace. The occurrence remains, but its event-character is disowned.

Not only are the narrative instances universalized, but occurrence is problematized. Christian narration not only tells what has happened, thereby fixing a tradition, but it also prescribes the *caritas* for what can happen, whatever it might be. This commandment orders the narrators and narratees to go to the forefront of the event and to make and carry out its narrative as if it told the story of a loving gift. Any referent can be signified as the sign of the good news announcing that 'we' creatures are loved.[12]

The hegemonic discourse of the Idea of love qualifies the event of the linkages to such an extent that descriptive and prescriptive phrases are necessarily joined together: considering that love (by legitimation from the origin to the end) led to the creation, and that the goal of creation is the realization of love, one must act (link) in a loving way. For God revealed in Jesus Christ that love is the origin and the goal of history. That Christ gave his life was the utmost expression of this love. This act of love can only evoke a response of love, as many verses from the New Testament affirm, such as Jn 15,9–17, resp. 1 Jn 3,16:

> [9]As the Father has loved me, so have I loved you. Now remain in my love. [10]If you obey my commands, you will remain in my love, just as I have obeyed my Father's commands and remain in his love. [11]I have told you this so that my joy may be in you and that your joy may be complete. [12]My command is this: Love each other as I have loved you. [13]Greater love has no one than this, that he lay down his life for his friends. [14]You are my friends if you do what I command. [15]I no longer call you servants, because a servant does not know his master's business. Instead, I have called you friends, for everything that I learned from my Father I have made known to you. [16]You did not choose me, but I chose you and appointed you to go and bear fruit – fruit that will last. Then the Father will give you whatever you ask in my name. [17]This is my command: Love each other.

> [16]This is how we know what love is: Jesus Christ laid down his life for us. And we ought to lay down our lives for our brothers.

All other discourse genres are subordinated to this: history, prayer, ethics, ritual, cognition, argument, etc. They always appear in the framework of the hegemonic discourse of the Idea of love, which forms the permanent background of all speech. People who do

not respect this background are unbelievers for whom there is no
salvation; those who step out of the narrative are heretics and/or
excommunicated. Both categories of people have therefore no right
to speak, since it is precisely one's being in the narrative that grants
one authority.

Gathering from Lyotard's observations, and in line with the four
characteristics of modern master narratives we have drawn from
his work, it is no longer difficult to see why Lyotard criticizes the
Christian narrative as a hegemonic, narratively structured discourse
of the Idea of love – that is, as a closed grand narrative. The
Christian narrative claims universal recognition as *the* discourse
to regulate the linkages. Stemming from a particular narrative
tradition, and therefore within a plurality of small narratives,
Christianity developed the 'virtue of love' to a universal rule. This
love, understood as a general principle, transcends the particularity
of traditional instances (addressors, addressees, . . .). The ground of
the commandment of love is the revealed primordial narrative of
the God who is love but who does not receive love from his children
in return. The commandment, revealed by God to all creatures in
the revelatory narrative, is formulated in a circular way: 'if you
are loved, you must love; and you will be loved, only if you love'.
Small narratives about sin and conversion function as examples of
this love. The instances of particular narrative traditions are thus
universalized.

6

Can God escape the clutches of the Christian master narrative?

It would seem that Christian faith is doomed to be enclosed within the structures of the master narrative, irredeemably hegemonic and unable to do justice to the victims it makes. The Idea of love appears to be the perfect cover-up for resolving differends through litigation. In Lyotard's writings, however, there are some fragments in which we can read initiatives that point towards otherness and disturb the Christian narrative from within. These initiatives, however, are concise – and are already clearly problematized at the site of their appearance. In this regard, there is little evidence that Lyotard, in dealing with the unpresentable, makes the 'theological turn' so many other philosophers of difference seem to have made in the past decades. In the following, we elaborate on both points, referring as much as possible to Lyotard's own words on these matters. We conclude by suggesting in what way theology might be challenged to transform itself, from *within* Lyotard's language pragmatic framework, into an open narrative. By doing so, we hope to show that such an understanding might both learn from and go beyond Lyotard's verdict over the Christian narrative.

Openings in the Christian master narrative?

Already in *Le différend*, Lyotard states that the *commandment of love* does not flow from the narrative itself (D234). The obligation happens: it is there, as a feeling in the one who feels oneself obliged, as a voice of conscience. And this obligation can turn the obligated one against the narrative.

> Inasmuch as it is a matter of ethics, obligation has, nonetheless, no need of an addressor, it is even to the contrary. At stake in it is: ought I to do this? The answer given the obligated one is that God wants it. S/he asks: is it really His will? The answer is that He declared His will at the beginning. The obligated one: but I don't feel it now, I don't understand what is prescribed by the authorized interpreters of the Scriptures, I feel the obligation for some other action (Joan of Arc's trial).[1]

In this regard, Lyotard speaks of the prophet referring to the one who resists the current narrative, sees him- or herself obliged to speak, and therefore is suspected and resisted by the narrative. For Lyotard, what is up for discussion – as would seem to be in the case of the prophet – is not the authority of the obligation but rather the authority of the narrative, the tradition itself. The sharp reactions of those who stand within the narrative against prophetism (and Lyotard avails himself of any reaction to the reformation, for example) betray the attempt to place the source of obligation in the hegemonic narrative and so to master the event of the obligation. Whoever sees him or herself obliged by *the event of the obligation* – the prophet – suspects the authority of the tradition.

> For his or her sake, though, the suspect [i.e. the one suspected by the narrative] holds the authority of tradition in suspicion. To belief (*sic*) in the narratives of love, he or she opposes faith in the signs of obligation. The latter is only actualized as the obligated one's feeling [. . .]. The authority of the commandment to love is not necessarily called back into question, but the repetitive, narrative mode of its legitimation certainly is. To judge that one ought to do *this* thing because that thing has already been prescribed is to defy the occurrence and the addressee's responsibility before it.[2]

And in a more technical style Lyotard adds that, in the feeling of the obligated one,

> narrative politics is shaken, including its way of receiving and neutralizing events, the communicability of addressors, addressees,

and heroes (referents) that is constitutive of community, etc. The deliberative concatenation, which welcomes the competition between multiple genres of discourse to signify the event, and which favors judgment over tradition, has more affinity with obligation than with narrative (which passes to the rank of fictive scenario).[3]

From a theological perspective, these remarks are not without importance. If God is the origin of the obligation, then the Christian narrative mortgages its possible openness by placing God in an unmediated way on the addressor-instance of the narrative. In this case, God belongs to the phrase universe; God is reduced to an element of the narrative. Such a God offers that narrative an absolute authority and necessarily results in the hegemonic closure of the narrative. In this regard, Lyotard speaks of tradition. The prophet, on the contrary, does not bind the authority of the obligation to the authority of the tradition (as a closed narrative), but experiences him or herself as obliged, as one upon whom a claim is made. Precisely in this claim, the prophet's narrative begins to endanger whoever sticks merely to the tradition.

We find another interesting reference to the Christian narrative, or at least to a Christian author, in *Moralités postmodernes*. Lyotard explains there the indeterminable, the unnameable, as *an other within the self* – another who is totally different from the others outside the self. This other has us in its grip and makes demands on us, and without our being able to make claims on it/him/her.

> But there is in this self another, whomever or whatever the self meets or seeks to meet during the hours of secrecy. This other exerts an absolute right over the self that was never contracted and is unaware of reciprocity. It is utterly other than 'the others.' It requires our time and our space in secret, without giving us anything in exchange, not even the cognizance of what it is, or what we are. We have no rights over it, no recourse against it, and no security.[4]

And, according to Lyotard, it was Augustine (with Paul) who first pointed to this internal division of the self by the presence of another which cannot be contained by the self.

> Augustine was the first, along with Paul, to reveal that inner split between the ego and the Other, who within the ego is deeper than the Other.[5]

For Augustine, this Other was the God of love who wanted nothing but good for him. This God, however, Lyotard comments, did not survive the 'deicide' executed in modernity.

In *Heidegger et 'les juifs'*, Lyotard is a bit more elaborate.[6] There he discusses the Christian narrative in the context of his thoughts about the 'Jews': the people taken hostage by the Other, by the God of the unreadable book, of the Law – for which the Jewish people in its wanderings is paradigmatic. In three different but related ways Lyotard refers to Christianity.

(1) In the framework of a discussion on the aesthetics of the sublime and the non-presentability of the unpresentable – concepts which, according to Lyotard, do not originate from the Greeks, but from the Jews and the Christians – he writes the following about the 'art of Christian preaching':

> How can one make felt the presence of the nonrepresented unconscious, if one limits oneself to the manipulation of 'figures,' made to persuade, and which can only be representational compromises where presence is figured and thus misunderstood? Aisthesis can only repress the truth of pathos (which is not pathetic) like the splendor of the church represses the presence of Jesus in the heart. Counter-Reformation, Jansenism, movement toward poverty in an effort to approach unfathomable misery. It is not Jesus' beauty that makes him true. He cannot even be approached through the senses; his incarnation is not his presence in the world, it is our tears sprung from joy. He is thus sublime, an insensible affection, a sensible presence in the heart only. How can the affection be present in the pulpit if the preacher only speaks of it? It is not up to him to make people cry. One cries in response to grace.[7]

Jesus is the name for the sensing of the event, not an objectifiable given that can be showed, represented or articulated – neither a word nor a phrase with a fixed place in a system. Whoever preaches bears witness to the sensing – a salient parallel with the sensing of the obligation just as this was earlier discussed.[8] That which Christianity is all about, is not locked up in a narrative. Grace as an event is not produced by the narrative.

(2) But it is also precisely here that Lyotard sees the *problematic paradox* in Christianity. Christians bear witness to descending

grace. The expectation of a new 'descent' of grace, however, is qualitatively linked to the (first) *incarnation*. Grace has already come in (the sacrifice of) the Incarnation of the word, and this opens the expectation of a new coming.

> A sign of love, this Pentecost testifies to and reiterates the sacrifice consented to by the Other (the Thing, the Unnameable) through representation, time, the name, desire, through flesh and death, so that the spirit escapes a little from the fast, from the deprivation of this absolute that it carries within itself, of that affection that it conceals, and from the anxiety that nothing will happen. But it has already happened, as passion, and it will not fail to happen again, as parousia. [. . .] It already happened that the unpresentable presented itself to the world; it will happen that it represents itself.[9]

The latter distinguishes Christians from Jews, according to Lyotard. It is their fundamental point of difference, and what is responsible for Lyotard's judgement that the narrative of the Jews is qualitatively more open than that of the Christians. Therefore Lyotard rejects the presumption of a Judeo-Christian tradition (with a hyphen) as if this would form one (seamless) whole. The expectation, the waiting, of a Christian is due precisely to the already happened Incarnation, a different waiting than that of the Jew. Grace presented itself in the Incarnation; a new presentation is expected, 'pre-dicted' in the already happened Incarnation. The Jews are still waiting.[10]

(3) Christians, therefore, integrate on the basis of what has happened.'They save the flesh and the earth.' In history, *reconciliation* is processed. That which the 'jews' are about, however, cannot be integrated. The reconciliatory dynamism of Christianity ultimately turns against the Jews. After all, the redemptive dialectics of the sacrifice succeeds in almost completely reconciling what happens in the world: for the benefit of the unreconciled, the Other has delivered his son ('représentant') to death, abandoned him and then taken him up again. This turns against the Jews when one wants to include what cannot be integrated within jewishness in a reconciling ('catholic', 'ecumenical') dialectics. Considered from a historical viewpoint, this dialectic resulted in obligatory conversion on pain of death, banishment, expulsion or destruction – and, in

our day, in making what is 'jewish' innocuous by the relativistic concept of permissive tolerance in contemporary society.

In 1993 Lyotard issued *D'un trait d'union*, which was completely dedicated to the *relation between the traditions of Judaism and Christianity*, expressed in the hyphen in 'Judeo-Christian'.[11] Lyotard also notes in this context that the hyphen separates what it intends to unite, and thus contributes to the forgetting of the 'jews'. Referring to Saint Paul, Lyotard writes that, because of the Incarnation,

> The truth of the Jew is in the Christian. Left to the letter, to his letter, the Jew is simply dead. Christian breath reanimates the letter, brings it back to life, gives it back its soul. The Jewish death thus becomes necessary and good, but only after the fact. A dialectic of repression? What is Jewish is what must be forgotten.[12]

In the dialectics of Christianity, the hyphen signifies the rupture with, or revolution of the Jewish tradition. In the remainder of this article, Lyotard develops Paul's dialectical line of thought by discussing justification and election, transmission, the flesh, law and faith, mission, the letter and the voice, Incarnation. It is in the Incarnation that the Voice becomes flesh, that the pattern of the alliance becomes manifest. With the Incarnation the Voice stops revealing itself in traces, in signs which have to be deciphered. And Lyotard concludes:

> Judaism is a struggle with the dead letter (what Paul calls a sign) and a struggle for the absent letter. The Incarnation is perhaps the revelation of the letter and, as a result, the revocation of foreignness.[13]

The Judaic tradition however is what history is about: not a dialectical hermeneutics, but a never-ending search. In Christianity this alienation has been reconciled by the dialectics of love:

> It is enough to want what the Other wants to say, what the Other means, to desire what it desires, to love its loving me enough for me to lose the love of myself; it is enough to have this faith in order to be justified, before any letter or any reading.[14]

Lyotard is right in pointing to the irreducible differend between the Christian and Jewish narratives. Likewise, the position that the openness of the Christian narrative is problematized by a dialectic (one that certainly appeared in history) of a too hasty reconciliation is not so easily refuted. Lyotard's discussion surely confronts the theologian with questions on the nature and meaning of incarnation and reconciliation, and the differend produced by them with regard to the Jewish narrative.

As an aside, we point to another instance in which Lyotard treats the place of the *Incarnation* in the Christian narrative. In *Moralités postmodernes* he briefly compares the Christian narrative with the Islamic narrative (on the occasion of discussing the Gulf crisis).[15] For Lyotard it is precisely the mystery of the Incarnation – the sacrifice of God's son – which enables the Christian spiritual community in its turn to be incarnated time and again in a concrete community.

> This was first political (the Roman Empire) and later economic ('protestant' capitalism).[16]

The result of such an incarnation in concrete form is politicization and dogmatization. Whatever goes against these historical incarnations is immediately interpreted as a humiliation of God, and not as an indictment of the vanity of individuals or the haughtiness of the community.

From what we read, it would appear that, due to its structure, Christianity inherently falls prey to the hegemonic features of a master narrative. The Incarnation definitively names and thus determines the event. Evidently, when asking whether the Christian narrative can escape the clutches of the master narrative, we will have to return to this suggestion at a later point in order to evaluate it from another perspective.

One last remark is given to conclude this section. In a text cited above, Lyotard writes that:

> it is not Jesus' beauty that makes him true.[17]

Witnesses of Jesus have been given more by a sublime experience than by a beautiful dogma. The analogy that Lyotard saw between the aesthetic and the historico-political thus may count as well for the religious. The relationship between the believing and/or theological word to the Word is not characterized by the (aesthetic) beauty of dogmatic systems but, rather, by sublime disquiet and powerlessness. A conclusion, though, Lyotard himself is not very eager to draw – something which distinguishes him from other thinkers of difference who do make the 'turn to religion'.

Hidden traces of God? Lyotard and the turn to religion in contemporary continental philosophy

Are there, at this point, theological and/or religious remnants to be noted in Lyotard – hidden traces of God? In other words, is the 'turn to religion', or the (according to some) 'theological turn', which seems to have permeated French contemporary philosophy, also recognizable in Lyotard's work?

At a certain instance, when dealing with philosophy's task to bear witness to the differend, Lyotard avows that perhaps we can learn from Jewish thinking: not to ask for an answer, but to ask in order to remain permanently 'in question'. Because, for the Jewish tradition, he continues, all reality is a dark message from an unknown, unnamed addressor.[18] Whether this statement, however, should be interpreted theologically remains to be seen – and certainly when one notices that, in the following, Lyotard refers among others to Levinas and Derrida. His calling upon the 'dark God' rather reflects the radical un(re)presentability of the differend, of the heterogeneity which accompanies and engenders the linking of phrases. Inasmuch as Jewish thinking then indeed can be considered as a discourse without a determined rule, it remains paradigmatic for the way philosophy should bear witness to the differend.[19]

Regarding religion itself, Lyotard is not at all convinced that it can heal the wounds of the twentieth century and prevent further calamity. Moreover, concrete religions often turn into master narratives that automatically regulate linkages (e.g. between cognitive and prescriptive phrases), and integrate whatever 'happens' from within their own narratives.[20] Lyotard's criticism of Christianity, which we presented in the preceding chapter, makes this point very explicitly.

Inasmuch as Lyotard has developed both a thinking of difference and an aesthetics of the sublime, however, there remains a striking similarity between his approach and other philosophies of difference, which, since the nineties of the twentieth century, are said to have made a theological turn, or at least a turn to religion.[21] In the attempt to overcome 'representation' and/or 'ontotheology', thinking difference in this regard has offered new ways to think transcendence as an irreducible otherness, as difference itself, and as heterogeneity. In order to deal with such thinking patterns, religion is no longer considered as a taboo but has been rediscovered as an important philosophical theme. Thinkers such as Emmanuel Levinas and Jean-Luc Marion have largely contributed to this development, but it is especially the work of the later Jacques Derrida, and the Anglo-Saxon reception of Derrida, which has made this 'turn' more pronounced, and has resulted in a deconstructionist (radical) hermeneutics of religion. For some of these protagonists of the turn to religion, the postmodern decentring of the modern subject coincides with an attempt to unfold the structure of religion itself, and it stimulates some even to develop a kind of philosophical religiosity.[22] Although Lyotard has developed very similar thinking patterns, it is difficult to claim that he himself explicitly made the turn. It would seem that rather for him, his mention of religion and religious language (e.g. with regard to 'the jews' and, as we immediately will see, to Augustine's *Confessions*) only serves strictly philosophical purposes: they are linguistic tools to express the structure of language, and to explain how to and why one should bear witness to the differend. Through such a procedure, a decentring of the modern subject is elaborated upon, resulting in a 'postmodern' philosophical anthropology of the 'fractured subject'.

However, similarities with protagonists of the turn to religion do include, for example, the appeal (and the urge experienced in the appeal) to bear witness to the differend; the apophatic strategies necessary for this witness to the heterogeneity involved in it; its irreducible otherness which both is the background of, at work in, and escapes from language; the evocation of the interruptive sense of the sublime; a sensibility for injustice and the ethical-political engagement to do justice (including the accompanying consciousness of its 'impossibility'); and, finally, the fascination for 'jewish' thinking. In all these aspects Lyotard's thinking patterns indeed resemble, for example, deconstructionism, and they further accentuate the urge not to forget conflict, plurality and heterogeneity, or to do justice. However, 'naming' the differend, and especially to name it as God, according to Lyotard, has led (and still leads) all-too-often to its forgetting. Also in this regard, Lyotard's position resembles the claim, for example, of Derrida,[23] to develop a thinking 'before' or 'beyond' negative theology, because the ambiguity of language (domesticating the event) is already and again at work in the latter.

In short, it probably does no justice to Lyotard to turn him into a religious or theological thinker. This being said, however, in view of the similarities with other philosophies of difference and their attempts to overcome ontotheology, his thinking at the same time opens up new modes of conceiving transcendence in terms of irreducible otherness, a process which might inspire philosophers of religion and theologians – even if Lyotard, due to his criticism of religion, would warn against the threats of domestication from the outset.

In order to illustrate this point, I will now turn to Lyotard's ultimate engagement with Augustine's *Confessions* in his unfinished and posthumous *La Confession d'Augustin* (1998).[24] Here again, Lyotard shares such a retrieval of the Church Father from Hippo with other thinkers of difference such as Derrida, and his intellectual offspring.[25] However, although Lyotard's work was written in the era of the so-called turn to religion, he makes it very clear that it should not be considered in the first instance either religiously or theologically. He presents Augustine's *Confessions* first and foremost as a witness of the differend – in this case, of the breach inscribed in the heart of the search for identity. According to him, the *Confessions* shows that the attempt to come to a complete surrender by confessing that one's life has been turned away from God ultimately fails. The 'I' never succeeds in coinciding with itself; there always remains an original distance which cannot be preceded or overcome. The confession always comes too late, he writes, and what has passed cannot be caught up with. The cleavage is not to be overcome; the breach is original.

> You, the Other, pure verb in act, life without remainder, you are silent. If he encounters you, the I explodes, time also, without trace. He [Augustine] calls that 'god' because that is the custom of the day, theology also being a work of custom. [. . .] Who can take the common measure of something incommensurable? A

form of knowledge that vaunts that it can do so, in bestriding the abyss, forgets the abyss and relapses. The cut is primal.[26]

Such knowing, then, forgets 'the grand forgetting', the always already being forgotten of the breach, the differend, the visit of the absolute. And here, for Lyotard, an all too quick and easy appeal to God in order to name this breach is again guilty of such a forgetting.

An analogous line of argument is made by John Caputo regarding Derrida's dealings with the *Confessions*. Regarding the genre of the *Confessions* as a prayer, he observes:

> From Derrida's point of view, the determinacy of the direction of the prayer is a way of trying to appropriate the secret, to make it one's own, to utter its secret name, revealed only to the believers or insiders, instead of confessing more radically its unknowability. [...] In that regard Derrida's 'Circumfession' is more radical than Augustine's *Confessions*. [...] For when Augustine confesses his wounded and mortal nature, he is also confessing/professing a faith in which these wounds would be bound up. But Derrida['s confession] is a confession without confession, a confession of the 'without'.[27]

In conclusion, Lyotard (as well as Derrida) refers to Augustine because of his struggle with difference, with irreducible otherness, at the borders of all meaning and identity. This is what Augustine calls God, but what at the same time escapes all determination, and goes under many names in postmodern thought.[28] Here, however, the question arises as to whether we, as Caputo stated, are really obliged to accept that such a postmodern confession would constitute a more radical confession than the one of Augustine, due to not naming God, not determining otherness, because of its being agnostic, and literally atheistic. Surely, it is another kind of confession, and perhaps such a postmodern reflection may assist us in understanding what confession is all about. However, it seems inappropriate to reduce Augustine's confession, however well intended this may seem, to such a postmodern confession, as if it would know better, as if postmodern thinking could reveal the underlying structures of religious consciousness, and of religious desire. In this regard, the criticism of Robert Dodaro is still in place.[29] For Dodaro, the Derridean deconstruction of Augustine's having been placed before God should be complemented with a deconstruction of the Derridean Augustine, who is thought of from an external relation to a finite god, and therefore condemned to a never-ending search. Indeed, Augustine's search for God is never complete, and marked by provisionality and contingence, yet testifying however to the continuing character of the conversion to God. If Augustine was the first to think the role of the subject in the search for identity, meaning and truth, and if his *Confessions* is exemplary for the continuing and undecidable stream of interpretation in which all searching for meaning and truth are situated, then one should acknowledge that Augustine did so from within an explicitly Christian-theological framework. It is definitely worth inquiring whether Augustine in his naming of God indeed fails, in line with the criticism of Lyotard, to keep open the breach in the self, or whether he nevertheless succeeds to do so in his own irreducible way, precisely *because of* God. Moreover, it would seem that the question can also be returned: one of the problems of the postmodern retrieval of Augustine is that the other manifests itself as a monster to which the subject is condemned, without escape, without mercy and without redemption.[30] However interesting a deconstructive reading of Augustine may be, it lifts the Church Father out of his primary Christian horizon of understanding, and such a reduction has its price, not only on the level of content but also structurally.[31]

The question thus arises as to whether we are really obliged to accept that Lyotard's 'postmodern confession' might constitute a more radical confession than Augustine's simply due to Lyotard's refusal to 'name' the visit of the other in the self, and by his relegating the name of God to the 'custom of the day, theology also being a work of custom'. With this remark, however, we now turn to the question of how a theological reception of Lyotard's approach and criticism may lead to a Christian narrative overcoming the hegemonic characteristics of a master narrative.

Lyotard and theology: Towards a Christian 'open narrative'?

How then indeed are we to engage Lyotard's philosophy of difference, his attempts to bear witness to the differend, and his criticism of the

Christian master narrative from a theological perspective? Is any Christian theology still possible after such incredulity towards the master narratives, including the Christian one? From the previous discussion we can retain at least *two major points of significance for a Christian theological engagement.*

First, regarding his criticism of Christianity, we might suggest that, even though Lyotard relativized the openings to which he referred, it is interesting to note how he pointedly criticized the Christian 'tradition' (D234). Lyotard finds that the Christian 'tradition' is a hegemonic narrative, legitimated by its beginnings, in that it identifies its addressor. However, at the same time, Lyotard points to the prophet who bears witness to the obligation, along with its unknown addressor, from which the commandment springs, and on *that* basis is critical towards the Christian master narrative. Could it be that a *discourse of the Idea of love is not necessarily to be identified as a hegemonic master narrative*? Could Christianity be a narrative in which the Idea of love is respected qua Idea? It would also seem that Lyotard's statement that 'it is not Jesus' beauty that makes him true', but that witnesses of Jesus 'take more after the sublime' allows one to look into the possibility that next to the analogy between the aesthetic and the historico-political (i.e. the language-pragmatic), the religious may also be structured analogously, thus capable of bearing witness to the differend.

Second, with regard to the turn to religion in contemporary philosophy, we indeed did remark that Lyotard never explicitly makes this turn, and therefore should not be identified with it. Nevertheless, inasmuch as his philosophy of the differend shares many similarities with thinkers having made the turn, the least one can say is that his thinking may offer *new ways to conceive of difference, otherness, transcendence, etc. without falling back into ontotheology, or, in Lyotard's own terms, into the hegemonic and self-enclosing patterns of the master narrative.* This narrative indeed closes when God (as love) is identified as the addressor, and love takes in all other instances. But can God be thought differently? Also, the question of whether Lyotard's 'confession' should be considered as the more original 'confession', finally, leads us again to the question of whether a non-hegemonic Christian narrative, in its own way bearing witness to the differend, can be envisaged.

For Lyotard, as we have seen, God did not survive the modern deicide. Moreover, today it is no longer the reconciliatory Christian

dialectics of love but the 'jewish' search without resolution that
sets the 'religious' paradigm for a discourse which forgets neither
conflicts nor injustice nor those victims who are often created by
our dealings with differends. The latter resembles more clearly that
which Lyotard was after in his language pragmatics: the feeling of
the impossible phrase. But is this the last word to be said in this
regard?

To continue our conversation, it is surely appropriate to bring
to mind, according to Lyotard, what the role is that philosophy
should play in the current age. At least it does not, as many of his
critics have ventured, tell the grand narrative of the end of grand
narratives (D182).[32] Philosophy is not the all-encompassing linkage
of phrases according to a hegemonic rule, but is a discourse always
in search of its rule. It is thus that he time and again strives to bear
witness to the differend. He suggests, in my opinion, that philosophy
is the attempt at a non-hegemonic, and thus *'open' discourse of the
Idea of heterogeneity*. The discourse of the witness to the differend
always remains under the differend's critique.

In the previous chapter, we have developed how, starting from
Lyotard's presuppositions, it can be plausibly maintained that
Christianity, including theology, functioned as a grand narrative, as
a hegemonic discourse of the Idea of love, yet leading to the creation
of both victims and injustice. This rather exclusive evaluation,
however, will not be shared by many Christians and theologians.
In the same way as many Christian thinkers *protest against a too
unilateral qualification of Christianity* in terms of ontotheology, an
unnuanced condemnation of Christianity *as a hegemonic master
narrative* will be met with criticism as well.[33] It is one thing to take
Lyotard's criticism to heart, and to criticize Christianity where it
indeed functioned and functions as a closed hegemonic master
narrative. It is quite another to *reduce* Christian faith to the latter.
Moreover, many Christians will take it to heart to bear witness
to injustice wherever this occurs and whenever victims appear,
especially if this happens in Christianity's name, not simply due to
the success of postmodern criticism, but precisely because of what
is sensed from within the Christian narrative itself – in Lyotard's
words: precisely because of the Idea of love, and the obligation
which goes with it.

In this regard, the claim that the Christian narrative identifies
the 'event character' of the event as what is already known from

the beginning, reductively naming it as 'grace', or a 'divine gift of love', is also reductive. In *Le différend*, as we have already said, Lyotard distinguishes between traditionalist and prophetic ways of handling the event – both from within a Christian perspective: the event of grace as the gift of divine love which calls forth an answering praxis of love (D234). Christianity in fact lives from the experience of grace, or better, from the event of grace, the gift of love. But Christians are all-too-aware that Christianity has suffered at many points in history from the incapacity to live up to this gift. As Lyotard noted, a too quick and facile identification of the event with the Idea of love leads to a Christian master narrative. But from a theological perspective, we ought to pose the question of *whether the terminology of grace in a sound theological discourse could function as the word 'event' does in Lyotard's discourse?* In other words, is not 'grace' a naming of the unnameable gift of love by the Unnameable, the One who is not merely part of the Christian narrative but who radically transcends it in principle (*Deus semper major*)? Certainly, the discourse receives a specific colour when the word 'love' is involved, but the critical impulses that the 'event' has in Lyotard's philosophy may well remain untouched. And this should not be forgotten: Lyotard also needs a vocabulary, phrases, and the linking of phrases, to be able to bear witness.[34]

If grace is the event of the breaking-through of God's love, then theology must critique every immediate closing of the event within closed narratives. The event of grace then does not function primarily as an affirmation of discourse strategies, a legitimation of the current Christian narrative, but rather it questions all speech, all linking of phrases, even the ongoing Christian narrative itself. Besides this critical aspect, *Christianity as an 'open narrative'* also contains a testimonial aspect: the experience of grace challenges us to give witness to it – knowing, however, that the event can never be encapsulated in our language. Because of the event of grace, the Christian is urged to retell the narrative of love over and over, and tell it in such a way that it bears witness to the ungraspable, unnameable and incomprehensible origin of the event of grace.

A further elaboration on Lyotard's language pragmatics may offer Christian theology the opportunity to come to a new, contextual self-understanding. Herein theological speech becomes aware of its *radical hermeneutical character*, fostering the consciousness that it needs to give witness to the event of God's grace. At the same time, it remains aware that this giving witness is context-dependent, never a complete nor an exhausting determination of what is not determinable.

Moreover, and this is a criticism ventured at Lyotard which he would potentially share with many proponents of the so-called turn to religion who develop philosophical negative theologies while trying to avoid the contamination of language: *maybe the incarnational approach of Christianity teaches us that narratives are always already told, and that language happens anyway, even in speaking about the impossible phrase.*[35] Maybe there are still other discourses which are able to develop themselves as an 'open narrative', while, at the same time, being aware of their own narrative structures (and the always imminent threat to recuperate the event), and which are called to openness – to let the discourse itself be interrupted by the event which occurs within every linkage to be realized.

*　　*　　*

In the following chapters we would like to continue our conversation with Lyotard in order to elaborate on the language-pragmatic and theological plausibility of such an enterprise. In Chapter 7 we will first engage the language pragmatic discussion, developing the language pragmatic plausibility of the model of the 'open narrative', as well as illustrating how this model may help theology to re-narrate itself as a Christian open narrative. In Chapter 8 we will discuss whether using a philosophy such as Lyotard's for theological purposes is in itself a legitimate project. In Chapters 9 and 10, we will finally illustrate how Lyotard's thinking patterns may inspire contemporary accounts of sacramental and political theology.

7

The language pragmatic plausibility of open narratives: Continuing the conversation with Jean-François Lyotard

At the end of the previous chapter, we suggested that the 'event of grace' may function in a Christian open narrative in an analogous way as the event does in Lyotard's philosophy. Such will result in a radical hermeneutical approach of the Christian narrative, which will first of all engender this narrative's critical consciousness, both with regard to the hegemonic tendencies in its own narrative and in other narratives as well. At the same time, such a hermeneutics should allow for an appropriate bearing witness to the interrupting event of divine love. In the present chapter we will further elucidate the language-pragmatic plausibility of our proposal. A first step in this endeavour is to enquire how we can better understand the nature of the discourse genre, and the way in which it deals with the linking of phrases coming from heterogeneous phrase regimens, and thus with the differend at stake in all language. In the first section of this chapter we will therefore have a closer look at the image of the archipelago Lyotard has presented to illustrate his language pragmatics.[1] On the basis of our conversation with Lyotard, we will argue that a distinction can be made between 'open' and 'closed' ways to deal with the differend, and consequently, in the second section, we will distinguish between hegemonic and open discourses. Afterwards we will elaborate on the differend itself, developing three distinct ways to consider it more specifically (i.e. under the aspects of conflict, plurality and heterogeneity). Finally, all of this will serve as an argument made in order to further develop the model of the 'open narrative' – a model which we propose to be retrieved in a contemporary theology which seeks to escape the clutches of the Christian master narrative.

On sea farers and the archipelago: Part 1

Lyotard offers the image of the archipelago in Le différend and in L'enthousiasme.[2] He presents it in a discussion of Kant's critique of (the faculty of) judgement, while appropriating Kant into his philosophy of phrases.[3] Lyotard first of all remarks that the faculty of judgement is not a faculty in the usual sense, because it does not, properly speaking, have an object, as do the senses, the understanding, and the faculties of theoretical and practical reason.[4] Indeed, the faculty of judgement is already at work whenever a phrase is evaluated as valid, and thus always already active in the midst of the heterogeneity of the phrases. It is precisely this omnipresence that enables the faculty of judgement to find passages between the different heterogeneous 'families of phrases'. After these remarks on the faculty of judgement Lyotard presents his image of the archipelago:

> If [. . .] an object must be presented for the Idea of the faculties' shifting gears if we understand them as capacities for knowledge in a large sense, that is, as capacities to have objects [. . .], and since the object suitable to be presented for validating the dispersion of the faculties must necessarily be a symbol, I would propose an archipelago. Each phrase family would be like an island; the faculty of judgment would be, at least in part, like an outfitter or an admiral who launches expeditions from one island to another sent out to present to the one what they have found (invented, in the old sense of the word) in the other, and which might serve to the first one as an 'as-if' intuition to validate it. This force of

intervention, be it war or commerce, has no object; it has no island, but it requires a milieu, namely the sea [. . .]. This sea bears another name in the introduction to the third Critique, that of field, Feld [. . .]. All [the] faculties find their object in the field, some carve out a territory, others a domain, but the faculty of judging finds neither one nor the other; it assures the passages between those of the others. It is more of a faculty of the milieu, within which all of the circumscriptions of legitimacy are captured. Moreover, that faculty is also what has permitted the delimiting of territories and domains and what has established the authority of each family over its island. And it has only been able to do this thanks to the commerce or warfare it fosters between them.[5]

Following this quote, Lyotard sketches a number of passages: the transcendental illusion (the awareness that a dialectic phrase in the form of a cognitive pronouncement is in fact non-cognitive); the beautiful as a symbol for the moral good (analogy); the use by practical reason of the scheme-structure of theoretical reason in order to apply the moral Idea (type). And he concludes:

Once more, then, the judge settles the legitimacy of claims to validity. In so doing, he slices the transcendental subject into insular faculties, and he trenches the field of all possible objects into an archipelago. But he also seeks out 'passages' that attest to the coexistence of heterogeneous families, and which allow transactions that are to the satisfaction of various parties. If the judge appears 'transigent,' it is because the judge is nothing other than the faculty of judgment, critique, and that critique can trenchantly decide only on the condition that it ought to be able to intervene in all the islands of the archipelago, only on the condition that it at least can 'pass' without any rule, 'before' rules, whether analogically or otherwise, in order to establish them.[6]

It should be noted that Lyotard here is concerned with *families of phrases* as an equivalent for what is called a 'faculty' in Kant. But both the definition as well as the examples of these 'families of phrases' remind us of what Lyotard means in *Le différend* with the expression 'phrase regimen' ('régime de phrases'), and not of a 'discourse genre' ('genre de discours'). The latter is defined there as the strategic linking of phrases from different phrase regimens for the realization of the discourse's goal. If this is so – and the text suggests this several times,[7] then all discourse genres function (if we apply Lyotard's pragmatics from *Le différend*) as sea farers, each of whom approach the islands with different strategies in order to reach their goal.

A correct interpretation of the image of the archipelago, however, is not an undisputed matter. The German philosopher, Wolfgang Welsch, for example, interprets the plurality of 'families of phrases' in Lyotard's image of the archipelago in *L'enthousiasme* with the plurality of 'discourse genres'.[8] It would seem that Welsch here is dependent on Richard Rorty's critique of French thinkers of difference in general, and Lyotard's image of the archipelago in particular. In that case, it may well be that Welsch has (uncritically) made Rorty's reflections his own.[9] Rorty's criticism itself dates back to 1985, to the French version of *Cosmopolitanism without Emancipation: A Response to Jean-François Lyotard*:

> Whereas Lyotard takes Wittgenstein to be pointing out unbridgeable divisions between linguistic islets, I see him as recommending the constructions of causeways which will, in time, make the archipelago in question continuous with the mainland.[10]

The first publication of *L'enthousiasme*, however, is from 1986.[11] Rorty based himself therefore on the archipelago-model as Lyotard developed it in *Le différend*. And what turns out to be the case in this context? There, Lyotard precisely means discourse genres when he identifies the islands (and thus the Kantian faculties). This is where we read – and we refer here to the French original version – in *L'enthousiasme*:

> Chacune des *familles de phrases* serait comme une île.

We find its parallel in *Le différend*:

> Chacun des *genres de discours* serait comme une île.

Lyotard thus corrects in *L'enthousiasme* the sentence from *Le différend*[12] because, here as well, 'discourse genre' is not the adequate term to point linguistically to the Kantian notion of 'faculty'. Lyotard defines the latter as:

> a potential of phrases subordinate to a group of rules for their formation and presentation.[13]

And, according to *Le différend*, this is precisely the definition of a phrase regimen:

> A phrase, even the most ordinary one, is constituted according to a set of rules (its regimen).[14]

It would indeed seem, therefore, that both Rorty and Welsch[15] adopt Lyotard's archipelago-image from *Le différend* without apparently taking the context in which this model is presented into account. They misjudged Lyotard's comparison of the islands (and thus the Kantian faculties) with discourse genres: this comparison is not only difficult to accept on the basis of the context, but moreover is problematized a bit further in *Le différend* itself where Lyotard explains briefly that neither the discourse genre nor the phrase regimen express what is called a 'faculty' in Kant (D187). In light of this comment, it is then very significant that, in *L'enthousiasme*, Lyotard in fact replaces 'discourse genre' with 'phrase regimen'.

Of course, this problem is entirely brought about by Lyotard's attempt to introduce Kant (and his adherence to different faculties) into the vocabulary and thinking patterns of language pragmatics, distinguishing between phrase regimens and discourse genres, a distinction that as such has no parallel in Kant. Every further development of the image of the archipelago, and thus every critique of it as well, must now take into account this difficulty. Therefore, in dealing with the image, we will stick to the distinction we made above between a phrase regimen and a discourse genre, and as such identify the islands with the phrase regimens and the sea farers with the discourse genres. The considerations that follow below will, we hope, support our option.

On sea farers and the archipelago: Part 2

In contrast to what Welsch seems to suggest, for Lyotard the plurality of discourses is not the most important feature of the postmodern condition, but rather it is the role these discourses play in the linking of one phrase to another, and the way in which they deal with its event-character.[16] After all, a phrase that has happened is claimed by a plurality of discourse genres, all of them presenting candidate phrases to effectuate the linking, and no meta-discourse is available to legitimately regulate the linking. Because linking is necessary but its specific nature is not, a conflict thus occurs between the diverse strategies and finalities of the competing discourses. This does *not* mean, however, as Welsch argues, that the linking is *always arbitrary*.[17] Each realized linking takes place from within the framework of the winning discourse genre: the linking is not arbitrary: not only is it very specifically regulated by the finality aspired at by this discourse genre, but it also happens because the latter has proven to be the more powerful one. What is important for Lyotard, however, is that a linkage dictated by the winning discourse at the same time provokes a sense of injustice with regard to the other discourse genres that could have put forward phrases to fulfil the linking as legitimately as any other. Because of his focus on the plurality of heterogeneous discourse genres, Welsch forgets the central place of the (happening of the) linkage: the differend. In other words, it is not the archipelago itself, but the sea that comprises the focus of Lyotard's attention. 'This sea is the linkage, both necessary and contingent.' For the status of Lyotard's 'travelling judge', this implies that

> one cannot not link on, one has no pre-established rule by which to do it, but *to establish the rule, one must link on*.[18]

Linkages always happen in the framework of a discourse, here to be sure a discourse without a set rule – but nonetheless a discourse.

But what then is the *difference* between, on the one hand, discourses such as the scientific, normative, aesthetic, economic or speculative discourse, and, on the other hand, *the discourse-of-the-judge*, that is, the philosophical discourse of Lyotard. With the latter also being a discourse, the question arises as to how philosophy as the 'discourse on discourses' can avoid being a meta-discourse. At least as far as Kant's judge is concerned, we have mentioned already how, for Lyotard, the faculty of judgement in Kant ultimately still functions with a supreme rule. In the end Kant turned all differends into litigations: his critical philosophy is embedded in a philosophy of the subject which is teleologically oriented towards the moral destiny of the person.[19] Or, put in the terminology of Le différend: all linkages occur within the hegemonic discourse of the Idea of freedom, and Kant's philosophy results in a modern master narrative of emancipation. Lyotard's philosophical discourse, on the contrary, intends to unmask such hegemonic discourses as totalitarian. Master narratives lead to terror and make victims because they negate the event. By strategically regulating the linkages, the event at stake in each linking is undone; the 'nothingness' 'after' the phrase that has happened is immediately filled up. The most powerful and thus efficient master narratives, furthermore, give the impression of respecting the event, of turning it into a pseudo-event which even engenders the narrative's power.[20] What is fundamental, therefore, is the question of whether, and how, discourses – and especially philosophical discourse – can pay respect to the event-character of the linking.

In line with what we already hinted at in previous chapters, Lyotard seems to suggest that there are actually *two ways of dealing with the heterogeneous plurality of phrase regimens and discourse genres*. Either one regulates all linkages between the different phrase regimens from the very beginning, thereby subordinating the other discourse genres as a result of either integrating their objectives into one's own objectives, or – in case this fails – simply suppressing them. This is the strategy of a *hegemonic* discourse. Or one attempts to constitute a kind of non-hegemonic discourse that does not forget the event immediately afterwards, strategically linking together phrase regimens and discourse genres. At least such a discourse, then, is aware of the fact that there is a differend to be respected, even if such ultimately is not possible because only one discourse is able to regulate. Such a discourse we would like to call the mode of a postmodern *open* discourse.

Let us now take up again the image of the archipelago and re-narrate it in this regard. As such, it would appear that, aside from the travelling judge, many others travel between the islands by ship as well, each one of them with their own intentions. One is a merchant and wishes to sell fruit from one island to another; the other is a gold digger, still another a soldier, or scientist, or pioneer, or mine worker, or thief, or revolutionary, or missionary. They all have their own plans and trace out their routes. For that purpose, they have the entire sea at their disposal. Their goals, however, are not the same. The anthropologist who wishes to study the original population cannot bear the gold digger who chases them away from their land. Just as the hunter is not happy with the forest development projects of the paper factory, and the merchant cannot get along well with the thief. In earlier times, it was different. The king went on an expedition – or organized expeditions in his name. And, on his ships, he assembled these individuals, each one of them with their own plans. He did not do this out of philanthropy but in order to pursue his imperial goals, to realize his own finality, his lordship over the sea, islands and subjects. That certain plans of his co-travelling subjects could no longer subsequently be concretized, or had to be adapted, was considered to be the price paid for the higher goal. Certain people were no longer allowed to take part anyway. Only those who were sufficiently submissive and servile to the king's plans could participate. But the king is dead now, and there is (still) a struggle for his lordship. Who will now determine where people are going to travel, and which island is to be visited first?

There is one co-traveller for whom it does not matter much which island is visited, but who loves travelling between the islands. The other travellers forget this travelling much too easily, he opines, because for them it is but a way of passing from one island to another – a necessity, but never the main issue, which after all is the island itself that fits in their plans. This one traveller is – rather reflectively and analytically – indeed exceptionally interested in the travelling itself, but at the same time pays attention to the archipelago, the islands and especially to his co-travellers. That interest is not based on a secret plan to lord over them; no, he likes to observe them, to see what is at stake, what happens. He studies what they do on the islands, where they want to go, how they want to determine the direction of the ship. He investigates to what degree they have reconcilable, if not opposed plans, where their boundaries lie, how they enter into alliances and make compromises, . . . Moreover, he sounds a warning wherever he observes that one of the travellers takes on the role of the king, takes possession of the islands, oppresses his co-travellers and commandeers the sea. Ultimately, however, he is very much aware of the fact that the travelling route is always determined, that one cannot go all of the possible ways, and that the feeling of travelling itself cannot be as such captured, but passes with time. Moreover, all-too-often he notices that new (sometimes very slowly creeping) ways of functionalizing the travelling manifest themselves, for example, through turning the sensing of travelling into a comforting pseudo-experience, forgetting about the event of what is at stake at sea – the production of travelling experiences for tourists of all sorts only being one example hereof. That is why he is very keen on remembering the conflictive nature of travelling; no route, no island, no destination, no purpose is given per se. He feels obliged to remind us as to what is at stake in travelling, and to present the impossibility of sticking to the event of travelling; he laments the always occurring forgetting of the event, and, even more, the forgetfulness of this forgetting. He looks for ways to bear witness to what 'really' happens in travelling, to present the event of travelling in its unpresentability, stretching existing vocabularies and discourses in order to find the impossible phrase, the route which cannot be determined, the destination which cannot be destined. In doing so, he finds delight, a feeling that he is after something ungraspable, but in a lot of cases he suffers from melancholia: he knows not only that it is never to be reached (for there should not be any reaching), but also that other discourses present themselves insidiously as surrogates, undoing the event-character of travelling by streamlining it in order to lead all travellers to their own purposes. Moreover, and this is worse, our most sincere attempts to bear witness ultimately may also fail, because they all-too-often forget what should never be forgotten.

Taking everything into consideration, Lyotard's discourse-of-the-judge still fulfils a privileged role and functions as a gauge for other discourses. Indeed, it is able to establish criteria to determine what are hegemonic discourses, and it can indicate from within its language pragmatic premises where master narratives have gone/are going wrong. Furthermore, it offers a vocabulary that allows for speaking about that which cannot be grasped in phrases; the event (formulated as a question: 'is it happening?'), or as was expressed elsewhere: the inhuman, infancy, the non-presentable, the indeterminable, or the quasi-referent of the Idea of heterogeneity. Moreover, Lyotard ascertains, without willing or being able to name the normative authority, that this sensibility for heterogeneity inadvertently obliges its bearers to bear witness to it. Sensing the event makes demands; estimating its non-presentability as something precious, and assessing its vulnerability mobilizes people to go against every hegemonizing, totalizing discourse. After all, for Lyotard, keeping heterogeneity open is about how to do justice, how not to forget that there are too many victims, and that all our discursive attempts to bring justice about all-too-easily make new victims. Discursive strategies which consciously aim at bearing witness to their own forgetfulness of the differend, therefore, are 'more just' than others. Furthermore, he admits in *Moralités postmodernes* that the postmodern world also narrates narratives about itself, even master narratives, that it keeps on narrating despite itself 'after the great narratives have obviously failed'.[21] A postmodern (open) narrative, which he himself narrates as a 'postmodern fable',[22] however, has nothing of a *modern master* narrative about it: postmodern narratives come into existence through the grace of those not yet filled-in spaces that a non-closed discourse keeps open.

Three senses of the 'differend': Injustice, conflictive plurality, radical heterogeneity

In the previous section, we rehearsed how Lyotard's postmodern thinking is not in the first place a theory of radical plurality but of heterogeneity. What is typical for the postmodern condition is not that we find ourselves in a condition of plurality, but in a situation where this plurality presents itself as conflictive. Factual plurality is the visible result of this conflictive discordance – or more properly: of that which lies at the basis of the conflicts, of that which reveals itself in the discordant plurality, that is, of the fundamental differend. This clearly distinguishes Lyotard's analysis of our current condition from Welsch's, but also from Rorty's. Both have applauded Lyotard for his analysis of the end of modern master narratives, while at the same time criticizing him for the solution he offers. They reproach Lyotard for focusing too much on heterogeneity and bearing witness to the differend, because, according to them, this would seem all-too-radically to problematize any discursive strategy or narrating, even those efforts which strive to deal with differends in non-hegemonic, open ways. In the following, we will further analyse *what is at stake in a differend*. By doing so, we hope to bring to the fore more clearly how Lyotard's insight into the heterogeneity involved in linking phrases may actually offer us a fitting starting point for further considerations on the intuition of an 'open narrative'.

When looking more closely at Lyotard's dealings with the differend, we can distinguish three different uses of the term, all in accordance with the nature of the context wherein Lyotard applies the term. We present *three dimensions of the differend* so that the perspective each opens up becomes progressively broader. Moreover, the first two dimensions ultimately refer to the third and more fundamental one. Consequently, we will treat the dimensions of injustice, conflictive plurality, and the radical heterogeneity of a differend, pointing in each case to the particular sensibility involved, after which we will indicate what bearing witness to the differend could mean in this respect.

The experience of the differend in its *first* sense appears as the experience of conflict – an experience particularly revealed in *not* being able or allowed to speak, to concatenate, to link onto the previous phrase. This occurs when differends are regulated as litigations. Phrases presented from discourse genres other than the regulating discourse genre are not allowed to play any part in the act of linking. More specifically, the differend can in this first sense be described as the situation of experiencing powerlessness and *injustice*. Respecting the differend here means searching for a language which is aware of this conflict and the injustice inflicted upon the victimized phrases/discourses, and denouncing attempts to silence other discourse, as well as the forgetfulness of the differend which goes along with that. One of Lyotard's examples is the differend the survivors of Auschwitz experienced through a statement Faurisson once made when he observed that these survivors cannot demonstrate the existence of the gas chambers, which discredits much of their narrative in advance.[23]

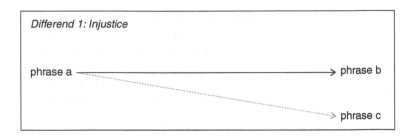

The *second* sense of the differend connects well to what we described as a differend in the first paragraph. A happened phrase opens up an expectation which is closed by a following phrase. Seeing, however, that no supreme rule is given to determine the nature of this following phrase, and that a multitude of phrases which are not reducible to one another present themselves to complete the linkage, a situation of radical plurality arises wherein no ultimate, harmonizing or unifying solution is present. The choice for one particular phrase necessarily excludes the actualization of the other phrases. The triumph of one phrase implies the defeat of others. Plurality cannot be radically respected. Even here, the accompanying feeling is one of powerlessness and an unavoidable injustice. In this case, respecting the differend implies regulating the linkage in such a way that the differend itself is referred to in the linked phrase – whereby it is made clear that only one phrase could follow, even if many other phrases were initially candidates.

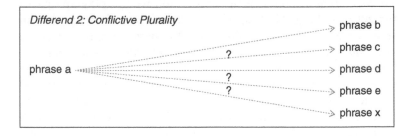

This second sense leads to a *third sense*. There is indeed something more to say. At the moment of linking, the linked phrase that closes up the expectation opened by the first phrase never comes to the point of satisfying this expectation. The second phrase does not succeed in signifying the indeterminacy, the rule-lessness, or the heterogeneity that separates the first phrase from the second. In fact, we can describe the other side of the relative nothingness of this 'moment' in-between phrases as an absolute fullness which can never be grasped or (re)presented in the concatenated phrase. If 'Differend 2' refers to the condition of radical plurality and the contingent and conflictive nature of the linking, and 'Differend 1' to the factual injustice that an imposed linkage causes to third-party phrases that are not actualized, then the more fundamental 'Differend 3' bears witness to the Idea of heterogeneity that accompanies every act of linking. In light of 'Differend 3', radical and conflictive plurality appears not as fundamental, but as a reference, a sign, or a hint at this Idea of heterogeneity. In other words, the inexpressible (inconceivable, non-presentable) accompanies all speech (conceiving, presenting), even invites us to speak, but is not to be identified with any articulated word or phrase (which implies that the term 'inexpressible' [inconceivable, non-presentable] itself also only refers to what cannot be expressed). There is plurality because no phrase can exhaustively present the inexpressible which asks to be expressed. Any attempt to do so disregards the conflictive nature of the radical plurality and causes an injustice to occur. Bearing witness to the differend in the case of 'Differend 3' means linking in such a way that the inexpressibility of the inexpressible is referred to. Here, therefore, the experience of the differend becomes the sensing of the impossible phrase: the sensing of the impossibility of the phrase which would succeed in expressing the inexpressible – the phrase which would succeed in articulating the event.

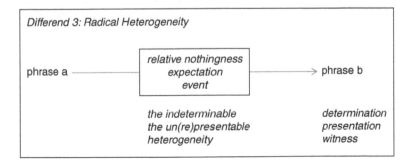

What then does Lyotard precisely mean by 'événement', 'il arrive', 'occurrence'? First of all, *event* stands for the occurrence of a phrase: a 'phrase happens'. Thus understood, the closure of a linking process is an event: the linked phrase happens. But here as well we can speak, along the lines of our considerations on the differend, of a more fundamental event that 'precedes' the happening phrase. We would then be dealing with what we have already indicated above as the expectation, the sensing of the impossible phrase, the experience of the relative nothingness between the happened phrase and the phrase to happen.[24]

The influence of Lyotard's aesthetic considerations is, in the case of 'Differend 3' (and the event in its fundamental sense), unmistakable. Here, his thesis that the aesthetic and the political – expressed by him in language pragmatic terms – are to be conceived of analogously, becomes clear. The sublime sensing of the non-presentable of the avant-garde is analogous to the sublime sensing of heterogeneity – the sign of history within the postmodern era. The 'now-moment' that the painter wants to entrust to the canvas is analogous to the event which the linked phrase intends to bear witness to. Just as the painter refers in painting to non-presentability, the philosopher bears witness in writing to that aspect of heterogeneity which cannot be grasped in phrases. Just as only a plurality of distinct commentaries can refer to that which modern painting is about – whereby these commentaries themselves are 'artworks' insofar as they also substantially refer to that to which the artwork refers – so also the event cannot be articulated in one phrase, or in one discourse, but is testified to by an irreducible plurality of phrases and discourses.[25]

Again, it is clear that Lyotard's critical view on postmodernity combines description with programme, and thereby attempts to strive for a maximum amount of openness with respect for that which in principle cannot be named, for what he calls an 'event'. However, his argument bears in itself its own relativization. Bearing witness to the event in the end also situates the event. For the indeterminable can only be referred to in a determined way. And apparently, several discourses can be deemed capable of having such a built-in openness.

The language pragmatic plausibility of an open narrative

In contradistinction to 'master narratives' or 'hegemonic narratives' – whether they be modern or not – the possibility of an 'open narrative' would seem to offer ways of dealing with differends which take into account a postmodern critical consciousness as expressed in Lyotard's work. Accordingly, discourses other than the discourse of the Idea of heterogeneity may be able to prevent an immediate closure of a narrative and to foster ways for a discourse to be opened up by interruptive otherness. At the same time, such a possibility not only seems in consonance with the language pragmatic settings of Lyotard's analysis, but also offers opportunities to adequately consider the very particularity of all bearing witness: one needs a lot of specific language to evoke what does not allow itself to be expressed in language. In the following, we will further elaborate on the concept of an 'open narrative', hereby developing some of Lyotard's intuitions, while at the same time continuing the language pragmatic results of the previous sections on sea farers and the archipelago, and on the three senses of the differend. We will first shed light on the category of 'narrative', then comment on the notion of 'openness', and conclude with some words on the twofold character of the linguistic practice of open narratives. In all three cases, we will point to the dynamic tension which ensues from the joining together of the words 'open' and 'narrative' in one concept. In the final section of this chapter, we will link our findings to what we brought to the fore at the end of Chapter 6 regarding the feasibility of a Christian open narrative.

Why *narratives*? In fact, we always keep on narrating narratives; we keep on linking phrases. These linkages – even the linkages that explicitly aim at bearing witness to heterogeneity – are not arbitrary, though they are indeed contingent. Sticking to the category of narrative puts the particularity and contextuality of every linkage and every discourse into better relief. A narrative offers the reason why, in the end, in all linkages, one phrase is chosen rather than another – whether the link is coercively regulated or not. Every discourse is potentially a narrative; it sets the pace effectively towards the level of the narrative at the moment that it 'ultimately' regulates the linking. After all, every differend is 'ultimately' filled in, or closed, when the linking is effectuated. To be sure, the wish for open narratives results from a historical development through which a critical awareness has been raised that hegemonic narratives – which in their own time seemed of the utmost plausibility and relevance – turned out to be disastrous. And this awareness is accompanied by the desire that justice should be done and victimization avoided. As a result, after establishing an incredulity towards modern master narratives, the only way left to be able to speak in a somewhat coherent sense seems to reside in problematizing this very coherence. Moreover, the impact and threat posed by the insidiously closed discourse of economization – which has meanwhile engulfed the political, technical-scientific, aesthetic, and other discourses – does not go unnoticed.

The category of narrative, therefore, reminds us of the *particularity* and *contextuality* of all speech. And this is also true for Lyotard himself. Why, for example, does Lyotard allude to the 'event' by appealing to Kant's aesthetics of the sublime? Or why is he using the 'inhuman' as a synonym for the indeterminable? What enables him to use it to criticize the nature and legitimacy of contemporary discourses on human rights? Or, more fundamentally, why is he concerned at all with the 'event'? The answer, however, is clear: because a discourse always consists of sequences of particular phrases strategically linked to each other. Such linking should not only be viewed in a synchronic but also in a diachronic contextual perspective. Goals and strategies are shown through the discourse's 'standard' sequences of phrases, particularly qualified contents and appropriated vocabularies, all of which have a history. Discourses bear the traces of their histories and are often present as (parts of) traditions within the contemporary linguistic field. Hence, Lyotard himself is inscribed within a tradition, as a matter of fact, within many traditions – as particular and qualified collections of phrases and discourses – in the context of which he develops his particular open narrative. Openness, then, is never an absolute achievement, a definitive characteristic of a discourse, but an on-going task, an ambivalent struggle that is not to be won, but only to be continued. In bearing witness, the risk, and even the temptation, to master the indeterminable is never absent. Time and again, a narrative that wants to be 'open' must cultivate this openness. Narratives, then, will differ in the potential each one of them has to open itself, attaining varying degrees of openness according to the nature of their strategies and goals, their structure, and their qualified contents.

When further elaborating on the *openness* of an open narrative, one could argue that an open narrative attempts, at the same time, to hold on to the perspective of the first and the third person, while involving them dialectically with each other. If we describe the first person as the narrative someone lives by, then the third person stands exactly for the reflexive moment, taking distance from one's own narrative. In their interwoveness which is constitutive for an open narrative, both perspectives relativize each other. The first person is relativized by the third person as one narrative among other narratives – and there are many narratives available. At the same time, however, the third person is never able to withdraw itself to an absolute and privileged observer's standpoint. Moreover, before the third person can tackle the narrative of the first person, it needs to be narrated. For there is no critique without a narrative, and this in a double way: only a narrative can be critiqued, and, critique itself takes on the form of a narrative. Or better: the confluence of critique and narrative is ultimately a narrative, a narrative that refuses to absolutize itself – that which consciously relatives itself, without, however, giving itself up. A pure first person would develop a grand closed narrative, imagining itself to be a third person. A pure third person would refuse to develop its own narrative, and thus would link to a position which is impossible. In other words, constitutive of an open narrative is a reflexivity which not only enables one to consider the narrative itself, but also refers beyond it, not to a more encompassing narrative, but to that which makes every narrative precarious. This reflexivity points to the breach in every narrative itself, produced by, and revealed in, the challenge to determine what is indeterminable.

At the foundation of this continuous perspectival change lies *an open 'habitus'*. The third person always recedes so that a synthesis of first and third persons becomes impossible. The position of the third person cannot be taken in as such. Openness can never be possessed, but is always to be strived for. The open narrative goes together with the accompanying sensing of the inexpressible in all that is narrated. It is the sensing of an immeasurable wealth, of endless depth, that asks to be set in words but always withdraws, like a horizon that cannot be overtaken. Despite all phrases and linkages, the indeterminable remains indeterminate. Every phrase always conceals a great injustice. Lyotard at times suggests that melancholy comprises the fundamental tenor of this sensing – quite understandable given the demise of the master narratives. But, on the other hand, one could also argue that there is a tenor of excess, of impervious wealth, that allows one (Lyotard, among others) to come to new narratives despite all instances of critique and melancholy. Therefore, it is not misplaced to state that the basic open attitude is intrinsically coupled to an explicit critical stance and praxis. Lyotard, for example, in his considerations on the non-human, bears witness to his conviction that the 'inhumanity' of the principally indeterminable is the only chance to escape the 'inhumanity' of absolute determination. The sensing of the indeterminable no longer allows for an assent to pure determination. Each attempt to close the narrative calls for resistance. The sensing of the indeterminable incites us towards the bearing witness thereof. This sensing of heterogeneity allows itself to be sensed as an ungraspable instance of heteronomy. One's own narratives are rid of their pretensions and referred back to their particularity.

From the aesthetic sensing of the sublime, wrote Lyotard, an 'élan', a 'Schwung' ensues. It compels towards *bearing witness*. After all, there must be a link. Given the necessity of linking, an open narrative is ultimately only left with the possibility of bearing witness via the nature of the linking, both formally as well as materially. For the linking of a discourse in search of its own rule is not arbitrary. The execution of this task will necessarily be contextually coloured, which implies that more than one open narrative is possible. Formal opportunities for bearing witness to the indeterminable are the strategies which no longer lean first and foremost on logical schemes, synthesis, deduction, induction, explication, reduction, inference, etc., but rather on opposition, complexity, irreducibility, paradox, paralogy, etc. But taking the material contextuality of the narratives into account may also help: neologisms arise, old words disappear, or are rediscovered. Their meanings shift, appearing in other contexts, etc. On this level as well, there is a potential to bear witness to the indeterminable.

Bearing witness thus takes place as a *linguistic practice*, as a linking, as an attempt to give expression to the relative nothingness by paradoxically filling it in. And this practice of the open narrative is engaged in a twofold way: on the one hand, its openness functions as an accompanying consciousness, on the other, it instigates explicit witness. Briefly one could suggest that, in reference to our previous section on the three senses of the differend, as a form of accompanying consciousness, an open narrative is occupied with the first two senses, and, as an explicit witness, with the third, more fundamental, sense.

First of all, an open narrative exhibits an *accompanying consciousness* that is at one point explicitly, then again implicitly, present in the linguistic praxis of the linking, and facilitates coping meaningfully with plurality. Once made explicit, three elements can be distinguished here. The accompanying consciousness is first of all a consciousness of *irreversible plurality*, of the insurmountability of multiplicity. Plurality is not so much seen here as a threat to one's own identity. Rather it makes one perceive that his or her narrative is one among many narratives, and that plurality provides opportunities for creative narrating. Second, it also contains the consciousness of the *threat of hegemonic narratives* to plurality: hegemonic discourses strive to neutralize other discourses in order to realize their own finalities. And the integration of an open narrative may be very attractive in this regard, because it would allow for the fashionable exploitation of its openness. Lyotard's analysis of the co-optation of a postmodern aesthetics of the sublime by the market is only one example hereof. Third, an accompanying consciousness includes the awareness that *conflicts* necessarily appear when phrases are linked – and this even without the involvement of hegemonic narratives. This implies at the same time that one is conscious of the fact that every linking could have been different, that ultimately no single phrase is capable of avoiding all injustice. In an open narrative, this threefold concomitant critical consciousness accompanies all linkages, setting out to keep the narrative open, and fostering the basic open attitude which is both its condition and source.

A second element, aside from this accompanying consciousness, is the inadvertent rise of certain attempts to give expression to that which is revealed within plurality and that which questions every hegemony: an *explicit witness*. By existing as such, an open narrative paradoxically strives to offer the language for that which has no language. Due to the accompanying consciousness, it tries, with full reserve, but nonetheless resolutely, to bear witness to the inexpressible which calls for expression. Acknowledging that it concerns itself with the discourse of the Idea of heterogeneity – itself a description of the indescribable – it professes its fundamental choice for non-hegemony. Put differently, the open narrative narrates the heteronomous instance behind all heterogeneity, the ever receding third person, the non-narrative, the non-linguistic, as the condition of possibility and source of all narrating, all language, and every act of speaking. The paradoxical character of the explicit witness lies in the fact that it refers, rather than represents. In so doing, it respects – in Lyotard's narrative – the Idea-character of the Idea of heterogeneity. It always leaves room for 'the other', knowing that this other enables and accompanies all discourse, while at the same time questioning it fundamentally. It intends that 'the other' has the floor, forgetting and respecting at the same time that this other has no voice, no language, no phrases and no determination – just as islands cannot encompass the sea, but the sea can indeed be named in reference to the islands that lie therein. Islands and sea farers bear witness to the sea, yet they are not the sea and do not master it.

In conclusion, open narratives are contextual and thus particular discourses embedded in a basic open attitude, constitutive for the identity of individuals, communities, and institutions, etc. On the one hand, they function as an implicit or explicit accompanying consciousness that regulates all linkages in such a way that their contingency remains affirmed; on the other hand, they bear witness to that which accompanies every discourse and tears it to pieces. They give expression to the sensing of radical plurality and refer to the ungraspable from within the contextuality of the discourse, using its particular strategies, standard sequences and qualified contents. And the reverse side of such an explicit witness is the praxis of the critique of hegemonic narratives – and, because a narrative tends to close in on itself, such a critique is always also directed to the narrative itself.

The language pragmatic and theological plausibility of a Christian open narrative

'The' open narrative as such does not exist. There are only particular narratives which can learn the lessons which can be gleaned from the recent past. This might also be true for the Christian narrative.

The question arising from the previous chapters and sections is therefore: can the Christian narrative reformulate itself as a consciously particular, and contextually embedded way of dealing with plurality and otherness?

Elaborating further on Lyotard's postmodern critical cons-ciousness, and as it attempts to bear witness to the differend, the model of the open narrative would seem to offer possibilities to critically engage the Christian narrative. In both *Interrupting Tradition* (2003) and *God Interrupts History* (2007)[26] we developed a theology serving the cause of overcoming the temptation of the Christian master narrative, and of contributing to the retelling of the Christian narrative as an open narrative. The category of interruption has been especially instrumental in this endeavour.[27] We have called upon this category to point to the difference or otherness which challenges the narrative from within. Interruption is what happens in an open narrative. It is not to be identified with rupture, that is, to end the narrative as such, because what is interrupted does not cease to exist. On the other hand, it also implies that what is interrupted does not simply continue as though nothing had happened. In both these books, we have tried, in dialogue with contemporary critical consciousness, to work on both the contextual plausibility and theological legitimacy of a Christian open narrative[28] – that is, to engage in a contextual-theological recontextualization of Christian faith.[29]

Dialogue with the contemporary context teaches Christians in the first instance that their faith is, culturally speaking, a *particular narrative* among a plurality of other narratives.[30] As such, the Christian narrative enjoys its own perspective on reality (the perception of which is irreducibly determined by this narrative from the outset): Jesus, confessed as the Christ, whose story, witnessed to by the apostles, teaches Christians that the mystery of reality is called Love. More concretely this means that, structurally speaking, Christians in our present-day culture opt for a specific narrative (including a community bearing this narrative) which is generally one among many. The Christian faith, moreover, cannot claim an absolute perspective since this would lead, of necessity, to totalitarianism.

A postmodern critical consciousness, resulting from modernity's self-criticism, reinforces this culturally conveyed awareness, and makes it more attentive to otherness and difference. Like all narratives, Christianity tends to close itself off from the challenge of difference and otherness. It threatens to become a totalitarian master narrative, immediately excluding or including otherness. There is always an otherness revealing the limits of our own position, and escaping every attempt to overtake it. There is always something unforeseeable, ungraspable, unexpected and unmasterable – something other – that interrupts our narratives.

Contextual plausibility, therefore, can only be gained when the Christian narrative structures itself as an open narrative. This is a narrative which has learned to perceive itself as a respectful, particular witness to radical otherness (apparent in the otherness of the concrete other) and develops a praxis of the open narrative (implying openness to the other, as a witness to the other, and self- and world-criticism). It is precisely here, in relation to otherness, that truth claims find their anchor: the truth of a narrative is then no longer a matter of true propositions, it is perceived according to the quality of its relation to otherness. In other words, the truth of the Christian tradition is bound to the authenticity of the tradition's stance towards the other. It should be clear, however, that confronting these aspects of the contextual critical consciousness has far-reaching consequences for the way in which narrative and community ought to function. This implies, for example, a Church which resolutely rejects, even internally, master narrative patterns, a Church in which narrative and community submit to the critique of, and constitute a multiform witness to, the God who, as the irreducible Other has made Godself known as Love. This brings us to the question of theological legitimacy.

While the fact that the Christian narrative should be an open narrative, can (and should) be motivated on contextual grounds, we nevertheless claim that this can only be done *legitimately on theological grounds* (i.e. in the narrative's own terms). The question therefore runs: does the structure of the open narrative also enjoy theological validity? Is it conceivable for Christians to understand the Christian narrative as witness to the 'other' who as an 'event' continually interrupts the narrative and challenges us to develop a critical praxis? What place does God have in such a scenario? At the end of Chapter 6, we pointed to the role which the event of grace could play in opening up the Christian narrative of the Idea of love. We asked the question, furthermore, of whether, from a theological perspective, the terminology of grace in a sound theological discourse could function as the word 'event' does in Lyotard's discourse. 'Grace' then would be considered 'the naming of the unnameable gift of love by the Unnameable, the One who is not merely part of the Christian narrative but which radically transcends it in principle'. God would then be understood as the Other who becomes visible in the concrete other, especially in the excluded other. God becomes impalpably revealed in the 'graced event' which interrupts our narrative. As the interrupting, open-breaking Other, God calls us out of our closed narratives and summons us to conversion, to open up our narrative for God's coming. Precisely because God does not have a place in our narrative, God becomes the driving force behind the critical praxis of openness, fostering forms of engagement which constitute a Christian open narrative. Indeed, it would seem that the other who challenges the Christian faith is not as such an external other, but may well *reveal itself from within Christian faith*. From within a Christian hermeneutics, the encounter with the other may be the place where traces of God become manifest. For has God not always been the Other of our religious narratives, especially when these narratives have threatened to close?[31]

It appears at least fruitful to use this perspective of *interruptive otherness* and its potential traces of God as a reading key. First it would seem that this *reading key* already fits the narrative given in the Old Testament. When Israel is enslaved and held captive in Egypt, it is God who, through Moses, breaks open this story of enslavement and alienation. When the Jewish kingdoms close themselves off from God and start to worship other gods, commit injustice to the poor and the strangers among them while kings become corrupt, it is God who repeatedly sends, on God's behalf, those prophets who criticize this closure. But the New Testament is also an account of a continuing interruption of closed narratives. Jesus forgives sins and heals the sick on behalf of God, opening new opportunities for those who, according to religious and social authorities, were outcasts. On behalf of the same God, Jesus criticizes those who reduce religion to the mere observance of the Law, or to a scrupulous making of the required sacrifices, or to a striving after merely political goals, etc. Jesus asks us to become like the children, like the poor, the outcast, and the persecuted (because they are blessed), like the widow who sacrifices her only penny. He invites us to follow in the footsteps of the father embracing his youngest son, and not to partake in the incomprehension of the older son. He teaches us to recognize him in the poor, the sick, the hungry, the thirsty, the prisoner, the naked, in short, in the vulnerable and wounded other. On closer inspection, the whole metaphorical dynamic of the Christian narrative appears to be permeated by the interruption, on behalf of God, of narratives, including one's own narrative, through a confrontation with otherness.[32] This is, for example, also illustrated in important motifs such as those concerning vocation, exodus, desert, mountain, cross, resurrection, conversion, pilgrim, etc. In no way is the Christian narrative allowed to close itself. For precisely then the God of love breaks the narrative open. Interruption thereby functions here as a *theological category*. Ultimately, the resurrection of the Jesus who died on the cross is the paradigm of interruption.[33] God interrupts the closing of Jesus' narrative by the religious and political authorities, and radically opens it. It is precisely here that God makes clear that the narrative of the one who lives like Jesus, professed by his disciples as the Christ, cannot be closed by or through death, but that such a narrative has a future *beyond* death. Following Jesus means engaging the challenge of the other who interrupts our narratives. It is through the encounter with concrete others that the Christian narrative is challenged and interrupted. And precisely this interruption could well be the place where God is revealed to Christians today. For, theologically speaking, interruption is not a formal, empty category, but is rather loaded with the narrative tradition of the God of love revealed in concrete history.

Even Jesus had to learn this, according to the testimony of the gospels of Matthew and Mark (Mt. 15,21–28; Mk 7,24–30). When Jesus moves to the region of Tyrus and Sidon, he encounters on his way a Canaanite or Syrophoenician woman, a non-Jew, who dares to ask him to cure her daughter possessed by a demon. At first, Jesus rejects her begging and claims that his mission only concerns the Jewish people ('the lost sheep of the house of Israel'). It would even be illegitimate to be occupied with others ('it is not meet to take the Children's bread, and to cast it to the dogs'). The woman, however, refutes his refusal, 'yet the dogs eat of the crumbs which fall from their masters' table'. At that instant, Jesus' narrative is likewise interrupted, and he learns to open his narrative further, so that others have their place in it as well. In the faith of the woman, God manifests Godself as also outside the borders of Israel.

Being a Christian as such calls one to *a praxis of both being interrupted and interrupting* – respecting the very otherness of the other while at the same time also becoming the other of the other, questioning and challenging the other, criticizing him or her where he or she tends to become hegemonic. The category of interruption in fact subsequently appears to be a good avenue to conceive of God's salvific engagement with history – including our involvement in history and the way we perceive God's relation to it. As a particular narrative, the Christian narrative is interrupted by the God it testifies to as the One who interrupts closed narratives, and, by doing so, is called to become itself a narrative interrupting closed narratives.

The past has seen a variety of approaches for theologically clarifying God and God's involvement with humanity. In a context in which belief in God is no longer evident as such, the conceptualization of God as the Other, as the One who always escapes and only comes to us as an unmasterable interruption, offers a conceptual structure which can help us come to terms with our actual condition. The fact that God does not have a 'place' in the Christian narrative but can only be evoked in God's ungraspability, prevents us from falling anew into the trap of totalitarianism.

The legitimacy of using Lyotard for theological purposes, however, has not remained undisputed. In Chapter 8 we will enter this dispute. In this chapter we will not only argue for the legitimacy of the exercise in which we are engaged, but shed light, at the same time, on the relationship between philosophy and theology, when engaging in theological recontextualization.

8

Lyotard and/or theology? On the precise relationship between philosophy and theology

For some theologians Lyotard's criticism of the master narrative of Christianity, as well as his anti-metaphysical (or post-metaphysical) bearing witness to the differend, would seem to be too critical and challenging. The dialogue between faith and reason would seem to get stuck within such a kind of reason.[1] Apart from the question of whether theology can profitably dialogue with Lyotard's thought, the entire discussion on the relationship between philosophy and theology is involved. On the basis of the proposals we have already made in the previous chapters, we now will take part in this specific discussion. To structure our argument, we will review, as a case study, the critical remarks of the German theologian Saskia Wendel as regards the appropriateness of a constructive dialogue between Lyotard and theology. Having devoted herself to a study of Lyotard's aesthetics in the nineties of last century,[2] she is not convinced that one can fruitfully receive Lyotard's thinking in theology.

Accordingly, in this chapter, we will first deal with Saskia Wendel's objections to a theological reception of Lyotard's postmodern thought. In the second section, we will argue against these objections. In the final paragraphs of this section, the dialogue between philosophy and theology within the broader fundamental-theological framework of 'recontextualization' will be dealt with.

Either Lyotard or theology:
Wendel's objections

The focus of Wendel's research is to enquire into this question: *how far does Lyotard's aesthetics of the sublime open up perspectives for theologians to speak about God.*[3] In such a context, Wendel first deals with Kant's conceptualization of the sublime, in contrast to his aesthetics of the beautiful, and then later concerning the reception of Kant's *Analytik des Erhabenen* in Lyotard's work. Subsequently, she wonders whether a surreptitious theology lies behind Lyotard's aesthetics of the sublime. She even sketches *four starting points* for such a theology – starting points that might tempt the theologian to identify the non-presentable (the sublime, or that which presents itself in the experience of the non-presentability of the non-presentable) with the divine, with God. First, she points to the partnership of pleasure and displeasure ('Lust und Schrecken') in the experience of the sublime, which reminds one, according to Wendel, of Rudolf Otto's conception of the 'holy' as a 'mysterium fascinosum et tremendum'. Second, there is the non-presentability of a (the) non-presentable, which could be related to mystical negative theology, and which would relate the sensing of the sublime sensitivity to mystical experience as well. Third, she suggests that Lyotard's considerations regarding the 'event' as a non-temporal now-moment might have reminiscences of an epiphany: 'the revelation of the divine in the moment, in the flash of the mystical experience'.[4] And, finally, likewise, the paradox between, on the one hand, the reaction to the event of an amazed and powerless silence and, on the other hand, the demand to give witness, can be fleshed out religiously as defined from an experience of mysticism. All of these starting points, as already mentioned, could result in the identification of a sensitivity for the sublime with the experience of the divine, that is, of the non-presentable with God. Lyotard would thus be recognized as the (philosophical) representative of the tradition of Jewish mysticism, just like other French thinkers such as Levinas and Derrida. As a result, postmodern thinking could be made fruitful for theology. Postmodern philosophy then no longer proclaims the end of theology, but offers new opportunities for its survival.

But are not such identifications and conclusions made too hastily in some sense? According to Wendel, theologians commit at least *two mistakes* when they proceed in this way. To facilitate our further discussion, we will number Wendel's criticisms, before attempting to respond to her conclusions. She first claims that in such theological approaches Kant's dealing with the sublime is misunderstood [1a], with consequences for understanding the sublime in Lyotard [1b]; and, second, that this misconception seriously affects the correct interpretation of Lyotard's dealing with the sublime [2].

> The religious interpretation of both the non-presentable and the sublime sensibility, according to me, is due, first, to a shortened explanation of the sublime already in Kant, which is then transferred to Lyotard, and also, secondly, to a similarly shortened interpretation of Lyotard's texts.[5]

Wendel, however, goes further in her rejection of the fruitfulness of Lyotard's thinking for theology. A modified reception of his aesthetics, within what could be called a postmodern aesthetic theology, is also dismissed by Wendel [3]. In order to make this dismissal, she cites three arguments: the specificity of Lyotard's aesthetic inquiry [3a], the absence of the question of meaning in Lyotard [3b] and the impossibility of a thinking through Lyotard's purposes together with the Christian concept of God [3c].

In the following, we will present the different arguments in Wendel's evaluation ([1a–b], [2] and [3a–c], respectively) and shed light on her critical reflections regarding presuppositions held by theologians who intend on integrating Lyotard's thought into theology. Afterwards we will provide a critical commentary and suggest corrections.

[1a] What do theologians do when they *interpret the experience of the sublime and the non-presentable, as brought to the fore in Kant, in religious terms?* According to Wendel, when the sublime is equated with God, these theologians either hypostatize the sublime feeling to a being, whereas for Kant it is purely about a subjective feeling, or they hypostatize the non-presentable – which is in Kant's view characteristic for the Ideas of the 'Vernunft', from which the non-presentability in the sublime feeling is revealed – into a non-presentable divine being. For Kant, 'God' is, to be sure, a necessary Idea of the 'Vernunft', but herewith nothing is said about this Idea's objective reality. *Or they do not ultimately respect what is intrinsic to the aesthetics of the sublime. The latter instead bears witness to the 'sublime in our nature', to the Idea of freedom and morality,

rather than to something that can be identified with the 'powerless religious subjugation of a people that bends its knees in worship before its Godhead'.

[1b] Wendel concludes: if theologians already misunderstand the thought of the aesthetic in Kant through their attempts to interpret it religiously, how much more do they *misunderstand the point of Lyotard's aesthetics of the sublime*. Lyotard is discussing the status of Ideas, as well, when he refers to the non-presentable.

[2] Moreover, in the non-presentable Lyotard is especially interested in *the event*, namely 'that it happens, that something happens'. His thinking is not about content, or significance, but about pure 'occurrence'. Lyotard does not enter into the question 'why is there something rather than nothing?', but into the question 'is there indeed something rather than nothing?' It is not the significance of being, but the being or not being of being itself, which is the focus of his question.[6]

To make clear what Lyotard is concerned with, Wendel directs herself – remarkably – to Lyotard's language pragmatics, his philosophy of phrases. By doing so, she hopes to demonstrate *the contingency and immanence of the event in Lyotard*. The event, after all, is the occurrence of a phrase and it is precisely this occurrence of the phrase as event that cannot be grasped in the phrase. The happened phrase can only negatively present the event, which 'precedes' the happened phrase, along with the presentation that happens in the phrase. This 'preceding' of the event cannot be interpreted as the non-presentable origin of the presentation, as a reality on the other side of phrase-events. Language has no origin, no expressible principle from which meaning ensues. Language as a unity does not exist, but rather only the plurality of phrases and the genres of discourse. And further:

> The non-presentable and absolute thus, in so far as it is the event and summit of Being itself, is not the One, the Universal, nor the Whole.[7]

Mindful of Lyotard's application of 'paralogy',[8] Wendel labels his philosophy – which is based on heterogeneity, contrast and openness – as 'paralogical thinking'. Such thinking can never be reconciled with traditional Christian theology and the metaphysical thinking patterns involved in it.[9] The event can in no way be understood as an epiphany, as a revelation of the divine. The non-temporal now-moment is only an epiphany of the immanent event. When Lyotard uses categories with a religious connotation, these function purely as 'analogies for a secular state of affairs'.[10] In short, Lyotard is neither a crypto-theologian, nor a philosopher of religion.

[3] But, given these conclusions, is it not thinkable that Lyotard, in a modified version, could nevertheless offer some inspiration for theology? One could aim, suggests Wendel, for a reception of Lyotard analogous to the way in which Marx's thinking has been received in liberation theology. Liberation theologians were not afraid to turn to Marx, while at the same time criticizing and correcting his atheistic presuppositions. Similarly one could revise Lyotard's thinking and construct an aesthetic theology on the basis of his aesthetics of the sublime. As was said, Wendel rejects such a reception on three grounds: [a] the distance of Lyotard from Kant (the primacy of the aesthetic), [b] the absence of the question of meaning in Lyotard and [c] the problematic definition of the concept of God.

[3a] First of all, Wendel returns to Kant.[11] With him, religion belongs to the field of ethics. The existence of God is not a theoretical matter but a postulate of practical reason. For Kant, the aesthetic is 'eine Vorstufe' to ethics and religion. Both the esteem one has for the moral law (and for God), as well as the religious mood, are considered by Kant as analogous to the sublime feeling:

> In the feeling of the sublime is announced aesthetically what is practically ensured. The sublime is, therefore, not only a praeambulum to morality, but to religion as well.[12]

From this it is clear, according to Wendel, that Kant's aesthetics of the sublime surely has theological relevance. This argumentation, however, does *not hold true for Lyotard's postmodern reception of the aesthetics of the sublime*, and this for two reasons: first, in Lyotard the aesthetic finality is no longer interpreted from the ethical (but the other way round); second, in Lyotard there is also no longer a ground for postulating a God. First of all, the non-deducibility of the ethical obligation (and specifically of the event as well) is also present in Lyotard. Both obligation and event go hand-in-hand with a feeling of esteem (as a negative presentation of the non-presentable, be it the law, or the event[13]). But despite this parallel between Kant's ethical law and Lyotard's event, both cannot simply be identified with one another. The law is homogenous and singular; the event, however, points to the irreducible heterogeneity of the genres of discourse. Moreover, the ethical in Lyotard needs to be interpreted precisely as it follows from the event:

> The ethical [...] corresponds not in the least with the homogenous law, but with the heterogeneous event.[14]

This leads us to the second reason: holding onto this irreducible heterogeneity precludes any possibility of ultimate reconciliation. Virtue and beatitude, however, demand the possibility of reconciliation. Therefore, given the absence of such reconciliation, the postulate of God is cancelled, because in Kant this postulate finds its ground precisely in the connection between virtue and beatitude.

[3b] A second reason to reject the theological relevance of Lyotard's thinking is the *conscious absence of the question of meaning in his philosophy*: Lyotard inquires into the possibility of being ('is it happening?'), not into the grounds of this possibility and thus into the meaning of being. Here, the theologian could blame Lyotard for two things, according to Wendel. On the one hand, Lyotard dogmatically excludes the question of meaning; in other words, he questions the possibility of being, without actually pondering the possibility of nothing. On the other hand, if it is impossible to point to a final ground which does not belong to the series of events, Lyotard is in danger of ending up in an unending regression of events. Wendel parries the first theological reproach with Kant: the one who is dogmatic is precisely the one who is not aware of the boundaries of knowledge and thinks he or she is able to demonstrate the objective reality of transcendental Ideas, in this case the Idea of God. As regards the reproach of an unending regression, Wendel admits that this does not disturb Lyotard but precisely seems to be an opportunity for a thinking that is paralogous and goes beyond established frameworks.

[3c] As a last reason, Wendel mentions those problems involved in the definition of God for theologians wanting to theologize with Lyotard. In this regard, she wonders whether God should be conceived of necessarily as unity, necessity, or origin; and whether God cannot be understood as event. Wendel adds that the Christian

conception of God has already been repeatedly exposed to criticism and its attributes have been questioned. She points for instance to feminist theology, in which the fatherhood, the omnipotence, the Aristotelian presentation of God as the unmoved mover, etc. are criticized. But such a critique does not go so far as to reject the conception (or essence) of God as unity, necessity or origin.

> From a Christian-theological perspective, the criticism of the traditional God concept finds its limits where the essence of the Divine is questioned. And precisely this happens when the definition of God as origin, a unity in Trinity, as transcendence in immanence, is cancelled.[15]

Theologians can possibly mitigate the identity thinking at the background of the Christian conception of God and make more space for difference (e.g. seeking alliances with Levinas), but they can never give up identity thinking itself. As a consequence, they will never be able to follow Lyotard. Theologians are posed with a choice: either theology, or postmodern thinking (à la Lyotard).

Receiving Lyotard in theology: On the relationship between philosophy and theology

According to Wendel, Lyotard's aesthetics of the sublime does not open any perspectives for theologians to pursue. In her evaluation, his work is not considered relevant for contemporary theology. It will come as no surprise then that we do not agree with her assessment. From the very beginning, and already in the way she poses her questions, Wendel problematizes any dialogue with Lyotard. In our evaluation of her position, (a) we will first treat the (too) important place which the thinking of Immanuel Kant enjoys in Wendel's discussion of the theological relevance of Lyotard's aesthetics. This will lead us to two deeper reflections, respectively concerning (b) her presentation of Lyotard's thinking (the place of aesthetics) and (c) the relationship between theology and philosophy, as this is implicitly contained in Wendel's argument. Where necessary, we will refer in our discussion to the numbers we have used to indicate the different arguments put forward by Wendel.

(a) To strengthen her argument, Wendel returns time and again to *Immanuel Kant*. She does this not only in order to shed light on Lyotard's aesthetics of the sublime, which is not misplaced due to the fact of the latter's dependence on Kant, but likewise to evaluate the theological plausibility of Lyotard's thinking. First Kant serves, so to speak, as the referee to enable her to impute a certain dogmatism to Lyotard's position [3b]. Wendel also employs him in order to make clear that Lyotard's aesthetics does not help in solving the question of God's existence. Kant's aesthetics is after all only a 'Vorstufe' of ethics and religion, and actually does not immediately – but only analogously – relate to the problematic of God; the sublime feeling cannot be hypostatized [1ab]. Even more importantly, seeing that religion in Kant is brought into the discussion in relation to ethics, and in Lyotard, according to Wendel, ethics cannot possibly lead to the postulating of God, there is no room for a theological reception of this aesthetics [3a]. In other words, Wendel continuously fleshes out the connection between religion (theology) and philosophy in a Kantian way: if one no longer meets the Kantian conditions in order to speak reasonably about religion – and this is apparently the case with Lyotard – then such thinking cannot possess any theological relevance. The least one can say is that Wendel's presupposition here is not self-evident, and this is due to two reasons. In the following, I will briefly mention these two reasons. Afterwards, I will further develop these two points as a second and third element of critique (b–c).

The first reason why Wendel's employment of Kant's philosophy as a referee is problematic resides in the fact that *Lyotard himself uses Kant for his own ends*. Lyotard teaches us to read Kant from his own standpoint, namely as a thinker of heterogeneity. Kant offers him the conceptual instruments to reflect on present sensitivities. So doing, by using Kant, Lyotard attempts to bear witness to the event. When theologians, engaged in processes of recontextualization, then wish to link up with Lyotard's postmodern thinking, it does not seem that the appropriate way to read Lyotard would be through Kantian lenses – but exactly the opposite. Moreover, Wendel's position has its own difficulties, which is shown by the awkward obfuscation of the importance of the reversal which Lyotard carries out in the relationship between ethics and aesthetics [3a]. If, in

Kant, aesthetics ensues as 'Vorstufe' from ethics (the sublime feeling ultimately bears witness to the greatness of the person, the Idea of freedom), then the experience of the ethical obligation receives, as Wendel also states, an interpretation analogous to the feeling of the event. If this is so, would the change introduced by Lyotard to the Kantian pattern not problematize in advance every attempt at demonstrating, from Kant, precisely the impossibility of the reception of Lyotard in theology? And is this not the case especially when one takes into consideration that the Kantian scheme – where aesthetics leads to ethics, and religion is thought of in relation to ethics – is abandoned by Lyotard himself?

Second, the preferential place enjoyed by Kantian thinking in Wendel likewise follows from *the relationship* she implicitly holds *between theology and philosophy* – and which brings her own argument again into difficulties. For whoever reflects on religion within a Kantian framework only extends primacy to philosophy: religion becomes 'Vernunftreligion', and theology receives its place only within the boundaries philosophy has set. However, it may be expected of those having read Lyotard's language pragmatics that they would respect all the more the irreducible diversity of the genres of discourse, in this case of philosophical and theological discourses. Even then it is still possible – with respect to this irreducibility – to speak of a mutual dependence. The ambiguity of Wendel's position is shown again when she, as a theologian, refers to the concept of God. Here she immediately derives this concept from the classical Christian-theological tradition and obviously forgets about the Kantian perspective (as regards, among others, the objective reality of God) she otherwise presented as normative [3c]. This move makes us at least pose the question as to the nature of the theological hermeneutics she wishes to employ.

But, as already mentioned, in our second and third point of evaluation of Wendel's position, we will now elaborate further on these two reasons and show why Wendel's Kantian slant hampers her assessment of the relevance of Lyotard's thinking for theology. We will first (b) contest Wendel's reading of Lyotard and afterwards (c) question her presuppositions concerning the relationship between theology and philosophy.

(b) *Wendel's perception of Lyotard* proceeds from his aesthetic philosophy. Her inquiry into the feasibility of a postmodern theology (is Lyotard's aesthetics theologically relevant, so that it is meaningful to speak of a postmodern theology?), makes it clear, moreover, that she does not go beyond his aesthetics. But, surprisingly, when she unfolds this further, she suddenly appeals to Lyotard's language pragmatics [2]. She uses the latter to clarify his aesthetic thought. In our opinion, however, whoever wants to investigate the relevance of Lyotard's thinking for theology would do better by proceeding the other way round and read Lyotard starting from his language pragmatics. After all, that is precisely where he develops his postmodern critique of the grand narratives (and thus also of Christianity). Precisely there he comprehensively sheds light on the phenomenon of the 'event'. And – in light of Wendel's preference for Kant – it is in his language pragmatics that Lyotard dissolves the philosophy of the subject through a philosophy of phrases. Hence, though exactly in the opposite way, we have opted to proceed from Lyotard's language pragmatics in order to unfold the significance and importance of the event. In a second step, we have elaborated on the 'event' as proceeding from Lyotard's aesthetic considerations – a procedure that is, for that matter, completely legitimate given Lyotard's thesis that the aesthetic and the language pragmatical, which equals for Lyotard the historico-political, are analogously constituted.[16] In light of this thesis, it is moreover surprising that Wendel holds onto the aesthetic perspective so exclusively and that she mentions the historico-political only fragmentarily, rather as a supplement to the aesthetic, while the former is not subordinated to the latter. Of course, the aesthetic is important for whoever wants to understand what Lyotard hints at with the term 'event'. At the same time, however, for a correct understanding of 'event', it is better – and for a possible reception in theology, more rewarding – to start from language pragmatics, in order to indicate there the crucial role of the event and, later on, to shed light on this term from the perspective of Lyotard's aesthetics of the sublime. Wendel's aesthetic exclusivism is all the more obvious when one observes that Lyotard's philosophy of the historico-political (the field of praxis) would have been more helpful for discussing religion from a Kantian (ethical) perspective. Most likely a majority of those who do not think in a Kantian way would prefer to situate religion within the historico-political. Finally, whoever proceeds from language pragmatics realizes, moreover, that the aesthetic is but *one* genre of discourse, while the historico-political is precisely the playing field of the genres of discourse, the field where linkages take place.[17]

Much more than in his aesthetics, Lyotard unfolds perspectives in his philosophy of phrases in order to reflect on the 'reality' present within language. As we have already pointed out, Lyotard there offers a way of thinking about transcendence and immanence in terms of otherness and difference. Indeed, Wendel is right when she says that the event is language-immanent [2]. But for Lyotard, that is also the case for the 'subject' (as an instance in the phrase universe). One, however, has to ask the question: what is 'language'? In the first place, it is a concatenation of phrases in genres of discourse whereby the linking is problematized each time, and betrays (reveals) something that is transcendent with regard to the happened phrases and regulating genres of discourse. Whoever stands open for the event feels propelled to bear witness to it and thus to develop an open discourse. Nonetheless, the event is never a phrase among phrases, or something to be traced back to a phrase, but always remains transcendent – even though it is 'language-immanent' – with regard to the preceding and following phrase, as well as with the genres of discourse.

Furthermore, whoever broadens Lyotard's thinking into a model of the 'open narrative', in contrast to the structure of the hegemonic master narrative, has the opportunity to deal with theology as a narrative – that is, in the area of the historico-political – alongside the philosophical narrative (Lyotard's open discourse). The latter's new way of reflecting about transcendence, then, not only becomes something with which theology is internally confronted but likewise something that questions theology from the outside as a different narrative. This brings us to the third element of our critique.

(c) *The relationship between theology and philosophy.* Why would theologians seek starting points for theologizing precisely in Lyotard? Are they seduced to do so only in order to be able to call themselves – fashionably – postmodern? And what do they look for in Lyotard? Wendel makes it seem as if Lyotard could offer theologians – as Kant did with his 'Vernunftreligion'? – a workable whole which enables them to practise their discipline. Or at least she gives the impression that theologians expect this from Lyotard. Wendel is certainly right in affirming that Lyotard initially does not provide this support nor that he even intends to do so. He is neither a theologian nor a philosopher of religion – and theologians cannot expect this of him. But does this settle the question of whether Lyotard can be made relevant for theology? Is the choice – after having read Lyotard – either to remain a theologian or to become postmodern?

Actually, Wendel offers the key to solve this dilemma herself. She points in fact to the methodological approach of liberation theology [3], especially to its interest in the Marxist socio-economic (and, in Marxist frameworks, also cultural) analysis-tool (as this took shape in historical materialism). What did Latin American liberation theologians look for in Marx? To be sure they did not attempt to appropriate his radical rejection of religion as the opium of the masses. They sought rather in his work for a method to bring their social context into an ongoing theological discussion, especially the methods detailing vast socio-economic inequality. In short, they wished to enable themselves to theologize plausibly and relevantly about the historico-political. These Marxist tools (already corrected by neo-Marxists) offered them the possibility for recontextualizing their theological discourses. A Marxist critical consciousness, which originally ventured a hefty critique of religion, challenged theology to recontextualize its own specific religious critical consciousness. As a result, this confrontation of theology with a Marxist critical consciousness did not lead to the sublation of theology, but gave shape to specific forms of Latin American liberation theology. This theology not only tested itself against this contemporary critical consciousness, but also criticized the latter within its own discourse.[18] What, then, do theologians look for in Lyotard? Not for an implicit theology (either negative or not) which they wish to develop further in their own name. They rather hope to encounter a plausible form of a current critical consciousness with which theology can confront itself to its own benefit. Lyotard offers the theologian a language for speaking about the historical-political (in this case, language).

Within this broader framework of the relationship between philosophy and theology, the problem of Wendel's theological hermeneutics also becomes clear. She ties down the God of the Christian tradition to concepts, like those that were developed in the recontextualization of the Christian narrative at the time of the philosophical dominance of metaphysics [2]. When Wendel then affirms that whomever no longer thinks of God as origin, unity, or identity, fundamentally does harm to the 'essence' of God [3c], this certainly raises serious questions from a methodological perspective in terms of recontextualization. During those times when classical metaphysics determined the frameworks of thought, metaphysics indeed helped give shape to the reflexive clarification of the Christian faith in God. But when one forgets the distinctness of theological discourse, that is, that the terminology and thinking patterns theology borrows from philosophy are applied only within the discourse of theology in order to refer to the God believed in, and when one wrongly thinks that these categories borrowed from philosophy (cognitively) describe the essence of God, then one opposes the hermeneutic consciousness that religion develops from its standing-in-relationship with the divine itself.[19] In other words, the metaphorical language that refers to what in fact is (still) not grasped in the current discourse – and God can never be grasped – is then literally understood and so loses all possibilities for making reference. 'God' then begins to function within a particular discourse as an instance of this discourse, and no longer as transcendent with regard to it. And precisely this is made clear by a theory of the open narrative which is grafted onto the postmodern thinking of Lyotard.

It is indeed the case that certain terms in the theological narrative have become established, as, for example, is the case with Father, Creator, Trinity, Logos, . . . (3c). But it is also important to note that these terms actually cease to function when they become merely part of the discourse. Such terminology should not be considered as a standard for rejecting every other language use that attempts to refer to God. One might better turn the relationship around. Such terms only retain their established status when their referential power is once again illuminate and restored by new references, or metaphors. Whether the referential power of the term 'Creator' is able to continue to signify God in our times by further interpreting this concept as 'origin' is, therefore, a pressing question. Perhaps, a perspective on the creative demand ensuing from the event offers better possibilities for referring to the being-creator of God.[20]

9

The interruptive event
of the sacramental

We will conclude our conversation with Lyotard with two examples of
how his philosophical thinking may inspire a constructive theology. In
Chapter 9 we will enquire in what way we can think sacramentality –
often conceived of from within pre-modern schemes – in a different
manner, and in Chapter 10 we shed light on how Lyotard may assist
in recontextualizing a late-modern political theology. In the current
chapter, we will first briefly introduce the question of how thinking
sacramentality has become problematic in a postmodern context.[1]
Afterwards we will hint at what a contemporary recontextualization
of sacramental thinking may result in.

Questioning sacramental thinking

Religious life, thinking and activity are basically *sacramentally
structured*. Every expression concerning God, whether in word
or deed, needs to be called sacramental and thus submitted to
sacramental theological reflection to the degree that it is inscribed
in, and gives form to, the mutual involvement of human beings
and God. In spite of the reception of modern elements into Roman
Catholic theology and Christian praxis, especially after Vatican
II, the prevalent sacramentological interpretation of symbols and
rituals used in the celebration of the Christian sacraments has
remained virtually pre-modern. The underlying idea was that the
holy or the sacred constituted a realm of its own, transcending

the mundane, and that this source of wholeness is accessible to us through the enactment of ritual gestures, images and words.

An unspoken but defining feature of this sacramental theology is *a neo-Platonic cosmology, or onto(theo)logy*. According to the latter, all creatures are ordered by the quality of their being, and can thus be located on a continuum flowing from God (*proodos / exitus*) and returning to God (*epistrophè / reditus*). The fundamental idea here is that of the *analogia entis*, a consequence of the emanation of beings from an original being. Although mediaeval theologians highly nuanced this neo-Platonic scheme (e.g. from the perspective of a theology of creation stressing the *creatio ex nihilo*), it remained the basic paradigm for understanding the relation between God and the world.[2] In such a theological epistemology, this neo-Platonic framework formed the foundation of theological knowledge. It is in light of this scheme that Thomas Aquinas' perspective on analogy has been generally received. According to Aquinas, we can justly attribute to God such 'simple perfections' as goodness, wisdom, etc. which are attributes borrowed from human experience and expression, because these perfections, according to the *analogia entis*, exist preeminently in God already before creation:

> Whatever is said both of God and creatures is said in virtue of the order that creatures have to God as to their source and cause in which all the perfections of things pre-exist transcendently.[3]

To be sure, negative theology does nuance the pretensions of this claim, but within the neo-Platonic scheme this does not change the definition of the onto(theo)logical foundation it implies. The logical order which human experience discovers to be discontinuous, because there is no univocity in speech about God, nonetheless reaches God, because that discontinuous *logical* order rests on a continuous *ontological* order. Within a neo-Platonic framework, the being of that which is caused depends first on the being of the cause, or source: hence, understood from the neo-Platonic basic paradigm, there is a background 'logic of the same'; ultimately theology is necessarily a homology. In this perspective, theological truth is supported by ontology. This same principle also holds for sacramentology:

> The sacramental event can be understood in neo-Platonic terms as the illumination of the single hidden origin in the 'being, living

and thinking' of contingent beings, an illumination through which these same beings become transparent to the primordial ground which shines through them.[4]

More specifically, sacraments function as events which bring believers into harmony with this origin, and do so in a reality which possesses a general sacramental structure because of the driving force which extends from the God-origin to beings, and therefore the transparency of those beings towards the God-origin. In such a context, sacramental grace is defined according to a causality-scheme: sacraments institute harmony with the origin. Sacraments, as a means of divine salvation for humankind, are not only the signs (*signum*) of grace but also what exercise or realize it (*causa*). It is in the sacrament itself, which 'causes/realizes what it signifies', that grace comes to us.[5] Sacraments stand in the *exitus* from God and they lead back towards God (*reditus*). According to Thomas Aquinas, God is the *causa principalis* of the grace that occurs in and through the sacraments (which can thus be defined as *causae instrumentales*). Only God, he says, can produce grace:

> as fire warms by virtue of its own heat. [. . .]. For grace, is nothing else than a certain shared similitude to the divine nature.[6]

As instruments, sacraments are that by means of which God produces grace.[7] Their original impetus comes forth from God.

As we have already mentioned, such pre-modern thought patterns *continued to determine much sacramentology and, more broadly, theology,* even after Vatican II. Reference can be made, for example, to the theology of Hans Urs von Balthasar.[8] The same principle is also operative in the theology of Joseph Ratzinger.[9] The latter is convinced that the dialogue between Judeo-Christian biblical faith and Hellenistic (neo-Platonic) philosophy has been providential. The world radiates from a more real and more intelligible reality remaining beyond the world, from which the world came forth and to which it returns. Our world is said to be sacramentally structured in the sense that it points transparently to the eternal. In this connection, Ratzinger speaks of the 'sacramental grounding of human existence':

> In the illumination of the world towards its eternal basic foundation, the human person also experiences who he or she really is: someone called by and to God.[10]

Sacraments aim consequently at the 'Einfügung in den durchgottete Kosmos' – the insertion within a divinized cosmos.[11]

Many modern theologians have reacted against this 'transcendence' of the holy and have rejected its pre-modern dualist, static and ahistorical conceptions, seeking instead those approaches *more attentive to modern sensibilities*. Yet here too, and despite modern accents, there is often an important, and implicit neo-Platonically structured ontotheological premise. Methodologically, many theologians in one way or another enter into dialogue with contemporary philosophy and human sciences. The anthropological foundation of the sacraments is one of the most prominent outcomes of this endeavour: they are often explained as rituals pregnant with individual as well as collective meaning. Often, however, the theological legitimation for this move is given through recourse to classic, albeit rejuvenated, ontological schemes. The theology of Karl Rahner, for example, which undertakes a unique but successful dialogue with modern philosophy and anthropology, rests precisely on such a classically structured basic scheme.[12] Rahner's transcendental theology presents a dynamized and subjectified (or personalized) reflection on the relation between God and humans in a fundamental way, thus opening a place for both the human experience of freedom and the sacramental event. Still, the self-communication of God as grace-filled presence appearing to a fundamental human autonomy must be understood within the framework of a neo-Platonic ontotheology. Attempting to conceptualize the ontological essence of the self-communicating God, Rahner writes

> that in this self-communication, God in his absolute being is related to the created existent in the mode of formal causality [in contrast with the efficient causality in which something caused is distinguished from the cause], that is, that he does not originally cause and produce something different from himself in the creature, but rather that he communicates his own divine reality and makes it a constitutive element in the fulfilment of the creature.[13]

God's self-communication, which is God's grace, is for Rahner an inner, constitutive principle of humanity given freely by God. Wherever people open themselves fully to God, the sacramentality of the whole of existence – the self-communication of God to the whole of existence – comes to light. In this connection, the sacraments are

> nothing else but God's efficacious word to man [sic], the word in which God offers himself to man and thereby liberates man's freedom to accept God's self-communication by his own act.[14]

Hence Rahner's modern sacramentological approach is carried out against a background which remains primarily classic.

Somewhat stronger modern accents can be found in the work of theologians who no longer focus on the human subject as such, but instead begin from its social and radical-historical rootedness.[15] For Edward Schillebeeckx, for example, and within the framework of a theological reading of the history of human liberation, the sacraments are considered 'anticipatory, mediating signs of salvation, that is, healed and reconciled life':

> So if it is rightly performed, there is in Christian sacramental symbolic action a powerful symbolic potential which can integrate politics and mystics (albeit in secular forms). In remembrance of the passion of Jesus Christ which was brought to a triumphal conclusion by God – as promise for us all – in their liturgy, Christians celebrate their particular connection with this Jesus and in it the possibility of creative liberation and reconciliation in our human history.[16]

Due to postmodern criticism, such patterns of sacramental thinking have lost a lot of plausibility, and philosophers and theologians such as Jean-Luc Marion[17] and Louis-Marie Chauvet[18] have proposed post-ontotheological ways of thinking sacramentality. Chauvet, for example, explains that thinking sacramentality within an ontotheological framework involving productionist schemes of causality (i.e. departing from foundational metaphysics) ends up in idolatry. He shares Heidegger's criticisms of ontotheology in remembering the ontological difference. Moreover, to proceed theologically, he claims that there is a 'homology of attitudes' between Heidegger's anthropological thinking and a contemporary theological anthropology. The relation between a human subject (Dasein) and Being is homologous to the relation of the believer to God. God's presence to the believer is thought of in a similar thinking pattern to that of Heidegger's thinking the manifestation of Being, which is also and at the same time the withdrawal of Being, that is, in revealing, God constantly withdraws. This positing of a homology in no way tends to identify the two; on the contrary, it implies that neither is reducible to the other.[19] Heidegger's account of *Dasein* and the Christian faith are both distinct ways of living, anchored within two irreducibly different, coexisting, symbolic orders. For, with Heidegger, Chauvet accepts that, due to the fact that Being has always already withdrawn, we are left, abandoned in a historically determined particular context. As such, we are embedded in a narrativity that is anterior to our identity; we belong to a symbolic order that irreducibly surrounds and determines us. Methodologically, philosophy serves theology both in situating the Christian faith in an anthropological and epistemological perspective, and in helping to express theologically what faith is. Philosophical clarification and theological motivation go hand-in-hand here: a specific and particular narrativity is developed in its normativity.

Sacramental differends?

In the same vein, Lyotard's thought both challenges and assists theology in thinking sacramentality. On previous occasions, we have already mentioned that the tension created by the constant and inevitable escape of heterogeneity from each particular attempt to give expression to it can serve as the basis for a reconceptualization of the dialectical relationship between transcendence and immanence, a relationship that is fundamental for the Christian tradition. The interwovenness of transcendence and immanence comes to expression in the dynamic interplay between the event breaking up the narrative and the narrative's witness to that event. The transcendent event continuously breaks open the immanence of the narrative, while precisely that immanence, in its effort of bearing witness, can define itself in view of that event. Accordingly, the relation between transcendence and immanence is not bi-polar, that is, thought of as two opposing layers into which all of reality is divided. Instead, transcendence is clarified as an ineffable moment of disruption or interruption in the midst of the immanent reality (of language).

This way of understanding transcendence is theologically fruitful and can prevent theology from becoming hegemonic. It dispossesses theological reflection of the possible pretense that it has made God comprehensible and given God a place within the immanence of reality. God is revealed anew in every event of heterogeneity – an event which, for theology, can be defined as the event of grace – though without implying a localization of God. The framework of postmodern reflection no longer permits us to think of God as occupying a localized position or site. In the grace-event, God becomes known as un-represented, hidden, ungraspable and incomprehensible, and always other, while at the same time opening up an expectation of a God who will come as the limit of, and break into, (worldly) time.

From this follows, when reflecting on the sacramentality of life, that here too, transcendence no longer denotes a pre-modern, neo-Platonic 'presence' or a modern, as it were Hegelian, 'identity'. In the postmodern context of plurality, transcendence is conceived of in accordance with the event of heterogeneity which confronts us with the particularity and contingency of our own (Christian) engagement with reality. Transcendence, as event, interrupts and disturbs the on-going particular narrative, challenging this narrative to open itself to the heterogeneity which breaks through in that event. The religiously experienced and interpreted relationship to the transcendent can thus no longer be conceived as a pre-modern 'participation' in salvific presence, or as a modern 'anticipation' of the ultimate identity. The Christian narrative, which has become conscious of its own particularity and contingency, can only adequately relate to the transcendent when it *opens itself up*, cultivating a sort of contemplative openness into which the transcendent as interruptive event can enter, and *bears witness* in a non-hegemonic way to the transcendent with help from its own (always fragmentary) words, images, stories, symbols and rituals. The sacramentality of existence does not offer us insight into some underlying foundational order, legitimating the existing narrative. Nor does it provide the redemption manifestly lacking in an unredeemed world. On the contrary, it opens up precisely that unredeemedness, that moment of interruption, to which no hegemonic narrative does justice. This sacramentality points towards neither an ahistorical ontological depth inviting human similitude, nor a history whose fulfilment is insured through a process of maturation, but rather the undermining of such self-assuring human constructions.

In this respect, the postmodern sacramental perception of time no longer reflects a pre-modern eternal continuum, in which the actual 'now' ceases to be. Nor is sacramental time embedded in a modern perspective of progress that cancels the 'now' in function of the future. Rather, sacramental time is the time of the interruptive, apocalyptic 'now-moment' ('kairos'), the event which opens up the particular and contingent, placing it in the perspective of the transcendent God, but without nullifying or cancelling its particularity and contingency. The event of grace, or the grace of the event, consists precisely in this: self-enclosed narratives are opened up, and this openness is remembered, experienced and celebrated. Living by this openness to what happens, narratives lose their hegemonic characteristics and become truly open narratives.

When sacramentality is understood in such terms, that is to say as the interplay of a continuous openness for the event of heterogeneity and an evocative bearing witness to it, then being a Christian can most adequately be described in terms of 'sacramental life and thought', and theology can be defined as sacramental in a double sense: as a reflection on sacramental life and thought, on the one hand, and itself as an expression of this sacramental (life and) thought, on the other hand. Theology, too, then reconstructs itself along the lines of an open narrative, standing in the continuous openness for what happens and bearing witness to this interruptive event. More specifically, such a theology is subsequently aware of the 'interruption' or 'disturbance' of the particular narrative through a confrontation with the open non-hegemonic Jesus-narrative. In this regard, Christian praxis as *imitatio Christi* will be focused on the option for the other, especially the excluded other, as a concrete incarnation of the Other.

Sacramental celebrations, as moments of the condensation of sacramental life and thought, are ritual gatherings where the fundamental faith convictions and insights of the Christian tradition are articulated metaphorically and expressed in symbols and symbolic actions. The basic metaphors of Christianity, which concern both creation and the incarnation, crucifixion and resurrection of Jesus Christ, are actualized in a testimonial and narrative way as the interruption and claim made by God, summoning us towards conversion, openness and bearing witness. From a Christian perspective, the Incarnation stands as the concrete marker of God's active involvement in the history of humankind. The paschal mystery (crucifixion, death and resurrection) forms the ground of hope for wholeness on behalf of a saving God; even in those experiences of unredeemedness, the hiddenness of God and God's 'present absence' reveal themselves. In each of the sacraments, in a particular way, this 'dangerous memory' is commemorated.

In summary, it is in order to regain contextual plausibility that theology must be able to take a certain distance from pre-modern and modern ontological foundations (as well as from the modes of legitimation offered by modern philosophies of history). The sacramentality of life, clarified and celebrated in the sacraments, is no longer considered as a form of participation in a divine being, nor as an anticipation of a self-fulfilling development, but as being involved in the tension arising from the interruption of the divine Other into our human narratives, to which the Christian narrative testifies from of old. Sacramental living and acting thus presuppose the cultivation of a contemplative openness and testify in word and deed to that which reveals itself in this openness as a trace of God. It goes without saying that such a recontextualization will have serious consequences for Christian self-awareness, and that such a sacramental structuring of human existence has implications which go beyond a theology of the sacraments.

10

The interruption of late-modern political theology

In this last chapter, we will offer another perspective on what may be gained for theology by furthering the theological conversation with Jean-François Lyotard. Here we will focus especially on the political theology of Johann-Baptist Metz and the dead-end to which this approach leads in the current context. After presenting Metz's project, and analysing its current flaws, we will show that a dialogue with the contemporary philosophy of difference, especially Lyotard's interruptive understanding of time, may offer a way out, one which not only safeguards Metz's many fruitful theological intuitions, but also restores the argumentative strength of the project of political theology.[1]

The interruptive aim of Johann Baptist Metz's political theology

According to Johann Baptist Metz, 'the shortest definition of religion is *interruption*'.[2] He formulated this statement as the sixth thesis in a series of statements on the apocalyptic nature of Christian hope. In the seventh thesis, he stipulated that the most important categories of interruption are 'love as solidarity' and 'memory as dangerous memory':

> a memory that remembers not only the successful but the destroyed, not only what has been actualized, but what has been lost.[3]

By accentuating the interruptive nature of religion, he wanted to make clear that Christian faith can never slip unpunished into a sort of bourgeois religion, seamlessly woven into the prevailing culture and society, nor withdraw itself from or against its context. Such religion seeks a too facile reconciliation, forgetting in the process the tragic suffering that confronts human existence. For Metz, there can be no Christian faith without tension or turmoil, without danger or menace. After all, Christians are bearers of the subversive, dangerous memory of the suffering, death and resurrection of Jesus Christ. By its very nature, the Christian faith disrupts the histories of conqueror and vanquished, interrupting the ideologies of the powerful and the powerlessness of the victims. Metz, therefore, advocates for a theology that is concretely active in history and society – a *political theology*.

Metz's theological critique is based on the *epistemological primacy of narratives of suffering*, interrupting the ruling paradigms of theological and philosophical thinking. In this regard, the *interruptive event of Auschwitz* is of a *paradigmatic* significance for Metz.[4] His criticism of Karl Rahner's transcendental-theological approach indeed bears on the pivotal question he addressed to his former teacher:

> Why haven't we heard you discuss Auschwitz in your lectures? Why is there little or no place at all for the histories of the suffering of people in our theologizing?[5]

It is the same question which fuels Metz's critique of Jürgen Habermas' communicative approach. After Auschwitz, theology is urged to take a stand against the traditional theological apathy towards concrete suffering and those paradigms of reconciliation that come too easily. Such a theological project therefore critiques religious, philosophical, and theological ways of thinking and living that omit, sublate, or eliminate the political and the historical: transcendental-idealism,

Marxism, positivism (with its technological variant), evolutionism, secularism, civil religion and eurocentrism. Metz reproaches them all for their subjectlessness and historylessness, their forgetfulness of suffering and of time.

Political theology, in this regard, should learn from the mistakes made by many modern theologies which, in their engagement with modernity, have taken on its aporias along with its valuable points.[6] Methodologically, Metz intends to arrive at a new hermeneutics of the Jewish-Christian tradition from a critical-productive discussion with neo-Marxist critical theory, pointing at the dialectics of the Enlightenment found within the works of such thinkers as Walter Benjamin, Theodor Adorno, Ernst Bloch, Herbert Marcuse and Jürgen Habermas. For Metz, such a dialogue should result in an *apologetic-practical fundamental theology*: both conscious of its standing within the dialectics of praxis and theory (praxis as the interruption of theory), and able to defend the Christian faith (its plausibility and relevance in particular) against modern systematic thinking.[7] Theologizing in this way can no longer start from system-concepts but should proceed from 'subject-concepts with a practical base': *memory, narrative, solidarity*. Instead of strong concepts, these notions are weak and fragile, and are mutually interrelated within a dialectics of theory and praxis:

> Memory and narrative can no more be practical categories in theology without solidarity than solidarity can give expression to the practically humanizing form of Christianity without memory and narrative.[8]

The result is a mystical-political theology that reflects on the praxis of the 'becoming-subject of all' before God, remembering God's option for this being subject of all as definitively revealed in Jesus Christ. It concerns an eschatological theology with a strong apocalyptic accent that is aware of the catastrophic character of time and the singularity and drama of the present within history. This should be a *dangerous theology* that implies the preferential option for the suffering and the oppressed, from the subversive but liberating memory of the suffering, death and resurrection of Jesus Christ. In this way, the Christian religion truly is an 'interruption', both in its self-perception (itself being interrupted in praxis, remembrance, suffering) and in its critical-active engagement within the world. In doing so, it practises a productive non-simultaneity with a modernity having become forgetful of history and the concrete human subjects involved in it.

The postmodern interruption of Metz's late-modern political theology

For Metz, postmodernity, as the result of the crisis of modernity, stands for the triumph of a generalized culture of *amnesia*. He blames this culture for cultivating forgetfulness, relativism, indifferent pluralism, anti-universalism and for adopting too easily the logic of the market.[9] He firmly rejects its *religion-friendly godlessness*, and what he calls 'polymythism'. In postmodernity, time has become an empty, surprise-less eternity. Religion is degenerated into a compensatory leisure-time myth without God and with Nietzsche serving as its great prophet.[10] More fundamentally, according to Metz, modernity entered its postmodern crisis because it forgot the *anamnetic depth-structure of reason*; the category of 'the remembering of foreign suffering' indeed founds a universality of responsibility.[11] Only in this way, for example, can the universality of human rights be legitimately held and maintained in today's cultural pluralism.[12] And it is religion, from its own anamnetic potential as a remembering and narrative community, which may offer modern society the interruptive memory that the history of freedom is also a history of suffering. Religion is 'resistance against such cultural amnesia'.[13] It is religion that offers a counterforce against the present cultural, empty endlessness and forgetfulness of time. From its apocalyptic consciousness, it remembers that our context is one wherein time is limited and determined – its end can happen at any moment. In this regard, modernity – and its praxis of becoming-a-subject-of-all – can only be saved 'within the horizon of the memory of God'.[14]

It is striking, however, that after 1985, in contradistinction to the period in which he developed his political theology, Metz almost completely *stops referring to contemporary critical theory and other thinkers as conversation partners* in order to develop his political-theological reflections. On the contrary, he firmly reproaches Jürgen Habermas for forgetting the anamnetic structure of communicative reason and severely criticizes postmodern thinkers of difference such as Jean-François Lyotard and Jacques Derrida, arguing that the 'linguistic turn' subordinates the being-subject of human beings to language and realizes the death of the human subject in the wake of the death of God, thus surrendering it to the relativism and indifference of nihilistic pluralism.[15]

Moreover, as an answer to postmodern amnesia and nihilism, Metz draws especially upon the *Jewish-Christian resources of Christian faith*, or better yet, calls for a retrieval of a de-Hellenized Christian faith. For, likewise in Christianity, the appropriation of the Hellenistic tradition rendered the Christian faith into a subjectless and historyless thinking on being and identity wherein ideas are more important than memories. Since its embedment into Greek thought, theology has lost its sense of time, suffering, remembrance and narrative. For in the Old Testament, Israel is still characterized as a people who do not allow themselves to be consoled by myths or metaphysics.[16] God was experienced, not as detached from time, but within time.[17] The imaginative perception of the world was framed within a temporalized perception of reality, 'in a horizon of a restricted time'. Likewise, in the New Testament – and surely in Paul – the perception of God and time is of the same import: 'Gottes Gekommensein ist im Kommen' ('God's having come happens in God's coming').[18] In its encounter with Greek thought, however, the biblical understanding of time was given up. The apocalyptic restlessness was discarded, eschatology was severed. The non-identity of God, revealed in the interruption of all thinking by (the remembrance of) suffering, was glossed over, and the biblical commandment against idols forgotten.[19]

Of course, a postmodern context, analysed so negatively in terms of amnesia, 'Unmundigkeit' ('tutelage') and so on, certainly does not seem to serve as a valuable dialogue partner in the same way late-modern neo-Marxist critical theory has proven to be for Metz's project. It is, however, worth questioning whether such a mainly negative, discontinuous evaluation of the current context does not in fact conceal the critical consciousness that is also available in this context and, for example, finds its reflexive expression in specific philosophies of difference. Metz indeed only focuses on the discontinuity between the Christian faith and its context in relating his theological project to the present context. From the perspective of recontextualization, however, it would seem that Metz *interrupts*

the process of recontextualization itself and is no longer able to deal
with the interruption the postmodern context provokes within his
late-modern political-theological paradigm. Put differently, while
certain of Metz's intuitions speak to the contemporary postmodern
context (and entail in one way or another some continuity with it), by
rejecting dialogue with postmodern thinkers he no longer succeeds
in reflexively clarifying these intuitions against the background
of the current context. The price paid for this is substantial. The
conception itself of what he understands to take place through
the use of the term fundamental theology is thereby at stake: the
effort to productively engage the critical consciousness of one's
time in order to come to an adequate and plausible apologetic. In
this regard, plausibility is always a contextual plausibility as well.
With his move backwards Metz puts the argumentative nature of
his theology at risk, a criticism of his theology that has been made
by Jürgen Habermas, among others.

By stressing the discontinuity within the context, the *context
ceases to be co-constitutive* for his attempt to recontextualize his
political-theological approach in a present postmodern context. As
a matter of fact, to answer the challenge of this postmodern context,
he proposes jumping across more than 1,900 years of Christianity
in order to link up with its Jewish roots. One may wonder whether
such a strategy is not comparable to the strategy of those Metz
labels as 'defensive-traditionalist' theologians. In response to the
crisis of modernity, which these defensive-traditionalist theologians
also analyse in terms of alienation and discontinuity, they do not,
however, retrieve Jewish-Christian origins but present the Patristic-
medieval, Greek-Christian paradigm as the solution: the marriage
of Jewish faith and Hellenistic thought, perceived by them as
providential, and characterized by a strong metaphysical-ontological
tint. One can therefore legitimately wonder if Metz does not commit
the same *hermeneutical mistake* which he blames others (like his
former colleague Joseph Ratzinger) for perpetrating: namely, for
putting a stop to the theory-praxis-dialectics in confrontation with
the postmodern context, in the same way as defensive-traditionalist
theologians have done in relation to the modern context.[20]

We can further ask why linking-up again with Jewish thinking
is necessary in this sense. Is it because the original form of the
Christian faith took shape here, for all times and even for today?
Or should we rather take it that it is precisely out of the aporias

of late-modernity that we (again) now have (more of) an affinity
with what Metz describes as the Jewish-Christian view on God,
history and the world? The second seems more plausible to us.
If this is so, then the current recontextualization of the Christian
narrative does not go back beyond the Greek-Christian paradigm –
no backwards recontextualization – but invites a new, postmodern
recontextualization in dialogue with current critical sensibilities and
thinking patterns. Perhaps only then, instead of simply projecting
this insight backwards onto its Jewish roots, the renewed discovery
of the interruptive structure of faith and theology may gain a more
profound contextual plausibility and theological legitimacy.

In the following, we will very shortly seek to recontextualize the
Christian faith and its political-theological interruptive structure in
the current context. This will result, on the one hand, in theological
self-criticism, but, on the other hand, also in opening up possibilities
to retrieve 'interruption' as a theological category. Such a retrieval
both opens up and continues the narrative tradition of the God of
love revealed in concrete history and society. We hereto enter, one
last time, into dialogue with the work of Jean-François Lyotard,
linking up his approach to Metz's apocalyptic intuition of time as
limited, and of history as conflicted.

Time: God interrupts history

Metz's question about how to do justice in situations of suffering
and irreconcilability is also the starting question of a postmodern
philosopher like Lyotard. The latter's criticism of modern and
postmodern master narratives bears precisely on the question of
who is allowed to speak and who is not: which discourses can
hegemonically master the linking of phrases, and, by so doing,
victimize other discourses? Lyotard's question is indeed how to do
justice in a context of conflict and injustice. Given the irreducible
plurality of the genres of discourses and narratives, he urges us to
be more conscious of the differend that occurs in all speaking – the
differend which cannot be annulled, but to which one can only bear
witness. Vis-à-vis Metz, and given the latter's criticism of Lyotard
and the linguistic turn, it is striking that Lyotard takes the history of
the suffering of Auschwitz as a paradigmatic starting point as well

(opening his 'more systematic' book *Le différend* with it).[21] Lyotard does not simply ask 'who is speaking?'; his opening question comes much closer – despite the primacy of language – to Metz's: 'who is not allowed to speak?', 'who experiences injustice in language?' It is the interruptive nature of language itself and our responsibility to bear witness to it (and especially the threat of its being forgotten in discourses and narratives), which is at stake for Lyotard.

In dialogue with Jean-François Lyotard, we first noticed that the Christian tradition and its theology often functioned along the patterns of a master narrative: Christian tradition and theology forget about the differends which remind us that, in both speaking and narrating, conflicts occur and otherness arrives. In criticizing Christianity's master narrative, Lyotard pointedly singles out Christianity's initial desire to craft a grand narrative of love by trying to harmonize all conflicts and occurrences. By loving the event of the differend, the latter is recuperated all-too-easily as the event of love – legitimating the narrative rather than interrupting it. At the same time, and here starts the theological recontextualization, critical-constructively engaging Lyotard's thinking patterns (considering plurality, difference, conflict and philosophy's task to bear witness to the differend) has inspired us to investigate whether the Christian narrative is doomed to be a closed, master narrative in and of itself, or, to the contrary, whether it is called by its own structure to constantly recontextualize itself as an open narrative. Lyotard's differential structure of language serves reflexively as such to express the revelatory and interruptive nature of the Christian faith and to conceive of the way in which the Christian narrative bears witness to this. Bearing witness to the event of love subsequently prevents the Christian narrative of love from closing in upon itself.

The advantage of engaging in such a conversation, moreover, also allows us to enlarge Metz's notion of interruption and thus the contextual field upon which a theology of interruption can be active. For Metz, it is particularly the confrontation with suffering that forms the impetus behind his search for a 'dangerous' theology of interruption. This confrontation compelled him – in keeping with his late-modern (neo-Marxist) dialogue partners – towards developing a *hermeneutics of suspicion* that turns itself against those narratives that too hastily reconcile and too easily forget. Today, however, a second opportunity presents itself. Along with the cultural interruption of the Christian tradition, Christians also find themselves confronted with (religious) diversity and otherness.[22] In this instance, a theology of interruption tends rather to develop a *hermeneutics of contingency*, which aims to maintain the radical historical and specific, particular, character of the Christian tradition, showing how precisely in this very historical and concrete particularity, God is salvifically at work. Indeed, the encounter with the concrete other may very well be the place where God reveals Godself today. However, such a hermeneutics of contingency, when correctly understood, includes a hermeneutics of suspicion. Whoever chooses to engage in contemporary dialogue with the postmodern context cannot ignore this theological lesson from the recent past. If not, the rediscovery of one's own identity and its boundaries in confrontation with the other will too easily slip once again into the facile closure of one's own hegemonic narrative. Yet again, the other quickly becomes the forgotten one: the one who hastily becomes enclosed by, or excluded from, our narratives. Religion can only legitimately be called interruption when it allows itself to be continually interrupted.

In short, for Lyotard, *time* is what is at stake in language: it is the philosopher's task to bear witness to the event of the differend, 'the now-moment' in-between phrases that is constitutive for discourses but can never be encompassed by them. It is this reflexive structure that assists us in reflexively retrieving the apocalyptic consciousness of the Christian faith, the realization that time is limited. Accordingly, it helps to conceive of Metz's warning against totalizing eschatological views that too easily forget the suffering and otherness occurring in the here-and-now of history. At the same time, it undoes Metz's retrieval of apocalypticism as a recessive effort at recontextualization, as well as overcomes its quasi-mythological features which impede the functioning of the notion of time as limited. The continual confrontation with what happens in the here and now, therefore, underscores the conflictual nature of time and of our ways of dealing with it. In such instances, God may reveal Godself, thus interrupting history and our narrative ways of dealing with it. Such revelatory interruptions, then, are constitutive of history (and our accounts of it), but can never be encompassed by it.

CONCLUSION

On the basis of our study it would be inappropriate to recuperate Lyotard as a religious or theological thinker. He is first and foremost a thinker of difference, attempting in diverse ways to bear witness to the differend, while criticizing the almost unavoidable forgetfulness of differends in our narratives. He especially warns against the injustice and victims caused by the all-encompassing and totalitarian modern and postmodern master narratives, who often knowingly and willingly include otherness within the narrative or exclude it from it. In this respect, Christianity, for Lyotard, is only one example of such a master narrative – and even one of the most successful ones, as it allows, in the name of love, to link to – and thus integrate – whatever happens.

For a Christian faith in search of understanding in the present postmodern context, however, Lyotard's philosophical intuitions and thinking patterns can prove to be very stimulating, when the theological task is understood in terms of recontextualization. Lyotard's philosophy fosters the development of a proper theological critical consciousness which does not only respond to his contextual criticism of the Christian narrative as a master narrative, but also enables the Christian narrative to retrieve from its own dynamics the resources for an open Christian narrative. Using the thinking structures of Lyotard to reread the Christian tradition, makes one attentive for the interruptive structure of this very narrative – because God interrupts – and renders one vigilant towards attempts to forget about such interruptions.

Similar to the way demonstrated in Chapters 6 to 10, other theological themes, approaches and authors may be dealt with using the thinking patterns developed from our conversation with Lyotard. As mentioned, such thinking patterns assist us not only in critically evaluating the state of affairs and the uneasiness with which much of theology relates to the current context. They also help out in reframing theological argumentative structures in order to regain contextual plausibility and theological legitimacy. They help us to see where theologies turn into master narratives and how to open up strategies of self-enclosure and exclusion of difference. They enable us to reconsider the Christian tradition as an open narrative.

Indeed, in particular theology can gain a lot from an in-depth theological appropriation, first, of the model of the open narrative and, second, of the category of interruption. In epistemological as well as political-theological ways, both have proven to be very stimulating for theological reflection. They foster in-depth and radical hermeneutical-theological ways of dealing with the Christian narrative, ways in which the consciousness of particularity, historicity and contingency do not threaten but qualify its truth claims.

At the same time, apart from being made fruitful in recontextualizing theology in the present era, the outcome of our engagement with Lyotard also positions us squarely on the field of contemporary philosophical theology. It enables us not only to delineate between fruitful and unfruitful ways of dialoguing between the two disciplines, but also stimulates us to contribute to the critical discussion of the so-called theological turn in recent philosophy. Instead of recontextualizing the Christian narrative in theologically legitimate ways, quite a few of these philosophical approaches seem rather to result in its evaporation.[1]

Both a further radical-hermeneutical engagement with the Christian narrative itself, its themes, arguments and authors, and a critical-theological discussion of the turn to religion in recent philosophy stand out as assignments to be taken up in the near future. We hope to present our results in this regard in a future volume.

ACKNOWLEDGEMENTS

A number of essays and contributions, published in journals and collective volumes, constitute the preparatory work behind this book. First of all, however, mention should be made of my already extensive conversation with the work of Jean-François Lyotard in my doctoral dissertation: *Spreken over God in 'open verhalen'. De theologie uitgedaagd door het postmoderne denken [Naming God in Open Narratives. Theology Challenged by Postmodern Thought]* (unpublished doctoral dissertation, KU Leuven, 1995). This work set the stage for further publications on this topic until today. In this regard, Chapters 2 and 6 have been prepared in *Jean-François Lyotard on Differends and Unpresentable Otherness: Can God Escape the Clutches of the Christian Master Narrative?*, in *Culture, Theory and Critique* 52 (2011), pp. 263–84; for Chapters 5 and 6, we also used *Theologie na het christelijke grote verhaal. In het spoor van Jean-François Lyotard*, in *Bijdragen. Tijdschrift voor filosofie en theologie* 55 (1994), pp. 269–95; and *Bearing Witness to the Differend. A Model for Theologizing in the Postmodern Context*, in *Louvain Studies* 20 (1995), pp. 362–79. An earlier version of Chapters 3 and 4 can be found in *J.-F. Lyotard's Critique of Master Narratives: Towards a Postmodern Political Theology?*, in G. De Schrijver (ed.), *Liberation Theologies on Shifting Grounds. A Clash of Socio-Economic and Cultural Paradigms* (BETL, 135) (Leuven: Peeters, 1998), pp. 296–314. In Chapters 1 and 6, reference is also made to my *Retrieving Augustine Today: Between Neo-Augustianist Essentialism and Radical Hermeneutics?* in L. Boeve, M. Lamberigts and M. Wisse (eds), *Augustine and Postmodern Thought: A New Alliance against Modernity?* (BETL, 219) (Leuven: Peeters Press, 2009), pp. 1–17. The third section of Chapter 7 is based on *Het 'geschil' van Jean-François Lyotard met Wolfgang Welsch en Richard Rorty*, in W. Derkse, A. Leijen en B. Nagel (red.), *Subliem niemandsland. Opstellen over metafysica, intersubjectiviteit en transcendentie* (Best: Damon/Radboudstichting, 1996), pp.103–17. The fifth section of the same chapter refers to material found in *Interrupting Tradition. An Essay on Christian Faith in a Postmodern Context* (Louvain Theological and Pastoral Monographs, 30) (Leuven: Peeters / Grand Rapids: Eerdmans, 2003), Chapter 6; and *God Interrupts History: Theology in a Time of Upheaval* (New York: Continuum, 2007), chapter 2. Chapter 8 rehearses the second part of *Method in Postmodern Theology: A Case Study*, in L. Boeve and J. C. Ries (eds), *The Presence of Transcendence: Thinking 'Sacrament' in a Postmodern Age* (Annua Nuntia Lovaniensia, 42) (Leuven: Peeters Press, 2001), pp. 19–39, while Chapter 9 refers to *Post-Modern Sacramento-Theology: Retelling the Christian Story*, in *Ephemerides Theologicae Lovanienses* 74 (1998), pp. 326–43. Finally, Chapter 10 is based on *The Interruption of Political Theology*, in P. Losonczi, M. Luoma-Aho and A. Singh (eds), *The Future of Political Theology: Religious and Theological Perspectives* (Farnham: Ashgate, 2011), pp. 53–65.

NOTES

Chapter 1

1 J.-F. Lyotard, *La condition postmoderne. Rapport sur le savoir* (Paris: Minuit, 1979) (ET: *The Postmodern Condition: A Report on Knowledge*, Manchester: Manchester University Press, 1984). He offers an interpretation of the term 'postmodern' with regard to what takes place in architecture, the philosophy of history, and art in J.-F. Lyotard, *Le postmoderne expliqué aux enfants. Correspondance 1982–1985* (Paris: Galilée, 1986), pp. 117–26 (*Note sur les sens de 'post-'*) (ET: *The Postmodern Explained: Correspondence 1982–1985*, Minneapolis: University of Minnesota Press, 1993).

2 J.-F. Lyotard, *L'inhumain: Causeries sur le temps* (Paris: Galilée, 1988), p. 13 (ET: *The Inhuman: Reflections on Time*, Cambridge: Polity Press, 1991, p. 5).

3 Lyotard, *L'inhumain*, p. 33 (pp. 33–44: *Réécrire la modernité*).

4 J.-F. Lyotard, *Moralités postmodernes* (Paris: Galilée, 1993) (ET: *Postmodern Fables*, Minneapolis: University of Minnesota Press, 1997); not without, however, clarifying now and then what he means by the term (see among others *Moralités postmodernes*, p. 89).

5 J.-F. Lyotard, *Discourse, Figure* (Paris: Klincksieck, 1971) (ET: *Discourse, Figure*, Minneapolis: University of Minnesota Press, 2011).

6 J.-F. Lyotard, *Économie libidinale* (Paris: Éditions de Minuit, 1974) (ET: *Libidinal Economy*, Bloomington: Indiana University Press, 1993).

7 He takes up some of the same lines of reasoning in his *La Confession d'Augustin* (Paris: Galilée, 1998) (ET: *The Confession of Augustine*, Stanford: Stanford University Press, 2000). In commenting upon this manuscript, Phillip Davis has remarked that in this book Lyotard goes back to Freud, talks about conversion as divine rape (a 'coming from behind'), and so forth. Moreover, *Libidinal Economy* is helpful for understanding Lyotard's 'anthropology' (though he would perhaps deny that he has one), especially as it relates to his later confession/re-presentation/etc. of Augustine's 'experience'. Also G. Bennington argues (in *Late Lyotard*, CreateSpace, 2005) that Lyotard invites the reader in *La Confession d'Augustin* to 'reconsider all his previous writing in an effort to bring together its apparently disparate periods and concerns': specifically, the early phenomenological work, the libidinal economy and his later childhood writings (p. 81). Bennington specifically mentions Lyotard's changed conception of time and the ability of Lyotard's phrase-based philosophy (*Le différend*) 'to produce an adequate analysis of . . . time'.

Bennington also quotes Delorès Lyotard saying that 'Lyotard always envisaged writing a "Supplément au Différend" which would extend its analyses'. Lyotard himself in this regard stated as well, 'But what is lacking in [*Le différend*] is precisely what matters to us here and that I am seeking (as a philosopher) to supply: *quid* of the unconscious in terms of sentences?' (*Late Lyotard*, p. 90, footnote 79). In light of the *Confession*, one could argue that Freud, received and interpreted by Lyotard as the libidinal, continues to be a force in Lyotard's thinking to the very end.

8 For the notion of 'recontextualization', see L. Boeve, *Systematic Theology, Truth and History: Recontextualisation*, in M. Lamberigts, L. Boeve and T. Merrigan (eds), *Orthodoxy: Process and Product* (BETL, 227) (Leuven: Peeters Press, 2009), pp. 27–44.

9 G. Ward (ed.), *The Blackwell Companion to Postmodern Theology* (Oxford: Blackwell, 2001).

10 See G. Bennington, *Lyotard: Writing the Event* (Manchester: Manchester University Press, 1988), pp. 6, 38; *Late Lyotard*, CreateSpace, 2005, for example pp. 14–16, 68–71.

11 See for example V. E. Taylor and G. Lambert (eds), *Jean-François Lyotard: Critical Evaluations in Cultural Theory* (London: Routledge, 2006), and also: C. Nouvet, Z. Stahuljak and K. Still (eds), *Minima memoria: In the Wake of Jean-François Lyotard* (Stanford: Stanford University Press, 2007).

12 See for example P. Jonkers and R. Welten (eds), *God in France: Eight Contemporary French Thinkers on God* (SPT, 28) (Leuven: Peeters Press, 2005).

13 See P. E. Davis, *St. Lyotard on the Differend/Difference Love Can Make*, in C. Dickinson (ed.), *The Postmodern Saints of France. Refiguring 'the Holy' in Contemporary French Philosophy* (London: Bloomsbury, 2012), pp. 123–37. Phillip Davis recently presented a doctoral dissertation at KU Leuven (Belgium) on how Christianity can overcome Lyotard's criticism that it is structurally a hegemonic master narrative of the Idea of love.

14 J. K. A. Smith, *Who's Afraid of Postmodernism? Taking Derrida, Lyotard, and Foucault to Church* (Grand Rapids, MI: Baker, 2006) (esp. chapter 3); C. Crockett, *A Theology of the Sublime* (London: Routledge, 2001).

15 G. De Schrijver, *The Political Ethics of Jean-François Lyotard and Jacques Derrida* (BETL, 236) (Leuven: Peeters Press, 2010).

16 Smith, *Who's Afraid of Postmodernism?*, p. 22.

17 Smith, *Who's Afraid of Postmodernism?*, p. 23.

18 Smith, *Who's Afraid of Postmodernism?*, pp. 68–69.

19 Smith, *Who's Afraid of Postmodernism?*, p. 70.

20 Smith, *Who's Afraid of Postmodernism?*, pp. 25, 72.

21 Smith, *Who's Afraid of Postmodernism?*, p. 73.

22 In this regard, he indeed operates in a similar fashion as, for example, John Milbank did, when announcing the project of Radical Orthodoxy. Milbank also appeals to the postmodern criticism of modernity, but only insofar as this allows him, in a second stage, to 'theologically reclaim the world again'. However, at this point it would seem that Smith parts ways with Milbank, for the latter consequently turns to the thinking of Augustine to conceive of a more original dependence of the finite to the infinite from within a Christian metaphysical framework, functioning as an oppositional master narrative against

the contemporary context, which he analysis in terms of modern secularism and postmodern nihilism. Cf. J. Milbank, *Postmodern Critical Augustinianism: A Short Summa in 42 Responses to Unasked Questions*, in *Modern Theology* 7 (1991), pp. 225–37; J. Milbank, C. Pickstock and G. Ward (eds), *Radical Orthodoxy: A New Theology* (London and New York: Routledge, 1999), pp. 1–20; J. Milbank, *The Programme of Radical Orthodoxy*, in L. P. Hemming (ed.), *Radical Orthodoxy? – A Catholic Enquiry* (Aldershot: Ashgate, 2000), pp. 33–45.

23 Smith, *Who's Afraid of Postmodernism?*, p. 74.

Chapter 2

1 Cf. Lyotard, *La condition postmoderne*, p. 11.

2 Comparable positions have been defended by Thomas Kuhn (*The Structure of Scientific Revolutions*, Chicago: University of Chicago Press, 1962) and Paul Feyerabend (*Against Method. Outline of an Anarchistic Theory of Knowledge*, London: Verso, 1976).

3 Cf. for example, J. Habermas, *Theorie des kommunikativen Handelns*, 2 vol.: I. *Handlungsrationalität und gesellschaftliche Rationalisierung; II. Zur Kritik der funktionalistischen Vernunft* (Frankfurt am Main: Suhrkamp, 1981).

4 Cf. Lyotard, *Le postmoderne expliqué aux enfants*, p. 9.

5 For a presentation of these criticisms, see Chapter 4.

6 Lyotard, *The Postmodern Condition*, p. xxv.

7 J.-F. Lyotard, *Le différend* (Paris: Minuit, 1983) (ET: *The Differend: Phrases in Dispute*, Manchester: Manchester University Press, 1988).

8 Published in J. Derrida, J.-F. Lyotard e.a., *La faculté de juger* (Paris: Minuit, 1985), pp. 195–236. Here Lyotard situates his Ideas in a direct manner in relation to Kant's thought.

9 J.-F. Lyotard, *Tombeau de l'intellectuel et autres papiers* (Paris: Galilée, 1984) (ET: Lyotard, *Political Writings*, Minneapolis: University of Minnesota Press, 1993).

10 J.-F. Lyotard, *L'enthousiasme: La critique kantienne de l'histoire* (Paris: Galilée, 1986) (ET: *Enthusiasm: The Kantian Critique of History*, Stanford: Stanford University Press, 2009). *L'enthousiasme* takes up once again a few 'notes about Kant' from *Le différend* in an altered form. Further: *Leçons sur l'Analytique du sublime* (Paris: Galilée, 1991) (ET: *Lessons on the Analytic of the Sublime*, Stanford: Stanford University Press, 1994); *Peregrinations: Law, Form, Event* (New York: Columbia University Press, 1988) (published originally in English; FT: *Pérégrinations. Loi, forme, événement*, Paris: Galilée, 1990).

11 For the present investigation, I do not consider the earlier work of Lyotard, such as: *Discours, figures* (Paris: Klinsieck, 1971); *Economie libidinale* (Paris: Minuit, 1975).

12 Cf. Lyotard, *Tombeau de l'intellectuel et autres papiers*, p. 61.

13 Many of his writings explicitly bear witness to this dialogue with Kant; see especially *Le différend*, *Judicieux dans le différend*, *L'enthousiasme*, *Leçons sur l'Analytique du sublime*.

14 The text of *Le différend* is divided by the author, 'in the manner of Wittgenstein', into statements, in each case provided with a number. References to Lyotard's text will be given according to these numbers, preceded by a 'D'. We will quote from the English translation: *The Differend*, here pp. 66–67.

15 The cognitive phrase regimen, for example, contains sentences which are formed so that they allow for a decision regarding truth or falsehood by means of verification/falsification, so that a possible consensus between addressor and addressee can be procedurally regulated (D28–30).

16 Transcriptions may well be possible: 'You must come outside' can be a transcription of 'Come outside!', but the original phrase as a phrase is not preserved in the transcription.

17 Lyotard, *The Postmodern Explained*, pp. 42–43.

18 Cf. Lyotard, *L'enthousiasme*, pp. 33–34.

19 We will deal further with this image of the archipelago in Chapter 7.

20 Kant brought Lyotard to this path by describing critical philosophy as the tribunal of reason where the judge passes judgement over the legitimacy of claims from various cognitions – which is transcribed in Lyotard's jargon as: the judge investigates the validity of the claims made by the different phrase regimens. In a litigation the judge passes judgement over a conflict between several parties, makes an appeal to an available law book, and uses the established rule – pronounces a 'definite judgement'. However, with a differend, there is no law book available, no rule to apply; rather, this rule must still be found, which means that a judgement must also be made over the rule itself – which is assumed by a 'reflective' capacity to judge. See Lyotard, *L'enthousiasme*, chapter 1.

21 Lyotard refers to P. Vidal-Naquet, *Les assassins de la mémoire: un Eichmann de papier et autres essais sur le révisionnisme* (Paris: La Découverte, 1987).

22 Silence is to be considered as a negative phrase which stands for that which unsuccessfully seeks to be expressed in a phrase. Such, then, is not possible because either addressor, addressee, referent, sense, or combinations of these instances, are neutralized through the fact that the differend is treated as a litigation (D22). One who survived the gas chamber, to take up the Auschwitz example again, may choose to remain silent for a variety of reasons: witnesses either think they do not have the sufficient authority to testify; or the possible addressees do not suffice; or, as Faurisson opines, gas chambers did not exist; or, finally, the absurdity of the event cannot be expressed in words – language cannot signify gas chambers (D24–27). To do justice to the differend in a situation of silence, thus calls for searching and allowing for new addressors, addressees, referents and senses; this also means recognizing that something asks to be set in phrases and suffers when this does not happen (D23).

23 Lyotard, *Judicieux dans le différend*, p. 229 (translation mine).

24 In each case, these stories are introduced and conclude with the presentation of the whole phrase universe: 'Here is the story of . . ., as I've always heard it told. I am going to tell it to you in my turn, listen to it! And this recitation invariably closes with another formula which says: "Here ends the story of . . . (Cashinahua name), or among the Whites . . . (Spanish or Portuguese name)."'

The stories themselves grasp on as the following: 'On that day, in that place, it happened that x . . .' and so refer to the particularity of the local story (Lyotard, *The Differend*, pp. 152–55 [*Cashinahua*], D222. For his information about the Cashinahua Indians he refers to A. -M. d'Ans, *Le dit des Vrais Hommes* (Paris: Union Générale d'Éditions, 1978).

25 Lyotard, *The Postmodern Explained*, p. 33.

26 Lyotard, *The Postmodern Explained*, p. 25.

27 Conflicts surface here. Stories from various communities collide, though not due to the existence of heterogeneous discourse genres – they all use the narrative genre, there is thus no question of a differend – but because of the incompatible diversity of names and meanings. There is, however, no judge, since there is no criterion to pronounce a judgement over all stories. The power of the story decides (D227): which is the better narrative? This power depends upon the degree to which the phrase realizes the goal of narrativity: namely to 're'-narrate the event by inscribing it in the development of the narrative itself.

28 At this juncture we cannot go into the technical discussion with Kant with which Lyotard engages. Regarding this, see Lyotard, *Le différend*, pp. 96–101 (*Kant 1*); *L'enthousiasme*, p. 25 and, for more context, *Judicieux dans le différend*, pp. 216–23. Lyotard defines an Idea as a universal concept, referring to an 'as-if referent' – that is to say, something that can only be presented as not presentable. For Kant, an Idea forms a concept to which no direct sensory intuition corresponds. It is a concept without any possible, perceptible, immediate presentation; it has therefore no cognitive value. Ideas are neither true nor untrue; only useful, usable, or unusable. Taken on in dialectical phrases, they function according to the rules of logic in an argumentative discourse that regulates the linkages by the mediation of something universal. Dialectical phrases strongly resemble cognitive-descriptive phrases; their concept demands, however, that they be treated only 'as if' they were cognitive phrases, as if they refer to objects set in time and space. Only an analysis of the phrase regimen and an inspection of the existing rules of validation can reveal their non-cognitive character. Kant would describe the treatment of dialectical phrases as would they be cognitive phrases as a transcendental illusion.

29 Such pretension indeed forgets the specific character of an Idea. The referent of the Idea of the emancipated proletariat is not presentable: it is an 'as-if-referent' to be used in dialectical phrases which only seem to be 'cognitive phrases'. In other words, the labour class as a totality cannot be presented as observable. This Idea can be attested only in signs, here for example in the enthusiasm that lives among labourers to change something about their situation. However, in Marxism, precisely this as-if character of the referent of the Idea was forgotten. Marx interpreted the enthusiasm of the labourers who wanted to take their fate in their own hands as a demand that ensued from the emancipated proletariat projected onto the future (D237).

30 Even if Marxism came to an end as a modern master narrative due to a loss of credulity, according to Lyotard it still goes on today as the sense of being entangled in a differend: that is the sense of being overruled and silenced by the totalizing subordination of all phrases by the rule of the capitalist discourse genre. Subjugated to the economic discourse, the discourse of labour is no longer respected for what it is in itself. Labourers are treated as merchan-

dise, or as owners of labour force. The consideration that labourers endeavour
to realize themselves through their work does not get a hearing. Within the
economic idiom, labourers only appear in the function of the labour force
they have to offer in relation to the demand, the value thereof transposed into
capital. In order to respect labourers as persons seeking realization, a different
language must be sought (for a more elaborate reflection on capitalism, see
Chapter 4). As already indicated, the traditional Marxist master narrative
also did not respect the differend, that is the diversity of discourses involved
in dealing with labour. It was the Party, which as supreme judge turned the
occurring differends about labour into litigations. For Lyotard's thinking
concerning Marxism, see for example D236–43 and 250; Lyotard, *Tombeau
de l'intellectuel et autres papiers*, pp. 23–31; *Judicieux dans le différend*,
pp. 232–35; and *Moralités postmodernes*, pp. 65–75.

31 In his 'note on Hegel' (in Lyotard, *Le différend*, pp. 137–45) Lyotard explains
that in the speculative genre, the referent is actually sublated by the identification of referent and sense; that which is said about the phrase is what is said in
the phrase: 'the Self is *in itself*'. At the same time, the Self takes in the instance of
the addressee: 'the Self is in itself *for itself*'. Thus referent, sense and addressee
are the same. Ultimately, the Self as the thinking that thinks of itself also takes
in the addressor-instance. Speculative discourse thus provides the conditions
which allow the Self to shift from one instance to the other. This discourse genre,
says Lyotard, affects this on the basis of three fundamental rules. First, the rule
of equivocation that states that each phrase needs to have the possibility of
presenting mutually different phrase universes. The second rule is the rule of
immanent derivation and always links as follows: if p, then –p; if –p, then p; p
and –p mutually imply each other: thus p and –p. The third rule is the rule of the
speculative result that prescribes that the transitions from p to –p and from –p
to p must be expressed by a third phrase in order to sublate the dilemma (and so
preserve it as well): if p, then –p, then q and as –p, then p, then q. The discov-
ering of the rules of the speculative genre, however, may give the impression
that besides the speculative genre, a meta-linguistic discourse would exist that
is precisely capable of describing the rules of speculation and thus shatters the
encompassing nature of the speculative discourse. However, when one looks
more closely, this formal meta-discourse works in opposition with regard to
the speculative discourse. And precisely because of this, it follows, at the same
time, the rules of the latter: speculation evokes non-speculation and vice versa.
Already from the very start, each opposition is recuperated in the speculative
discourse. The discovery of the speculative genre of discourse – as a result –
alongside other discourses constitutes itself as a reflexive moment in the development of the Self. There is no exteriority: the object of thinking is thinking itself
as it objectifies both itself and the object that thinks itself. Beginning and end,
goal and origin are the same; the first phrase is the last, the last the first.

32 Compare D152–60; Lyotard, *Le postmoderne expliqué aux enfants*,
pp. 38–40, 123. Following Adorno, Lyotard refers to the paradigmatic power
of the event 'Auschwitz': in Auschwitz, the speculative discourse is broken.
Auschwitz is not a 'speculative name'; it is not an objection that can be recuperated in a higher third, but rather a linguistic experience that calls the speculative discourse to a halt. After Auschwitz there is no 'result'. There is no more

'we' that can call itself Auschwitz, no more addressor, no more addressee, only a referent. It is the splitting of the Self.

33 For this: *Le postmoderne expliqué aux enfants*, p. 53; D257 and *L'enthousiasme*, pp. 108–9.

34 Lyotard, *The Postmodern Explained*, pp. 95–96.

35 Cf. among others: Lyotard, *Le postmoderne expliqué aux enfants*, pp. 38–39, against: Habermas, *Die Moderne – ein unvollendetes Projekt (1980)*.

36 See the fourth 'note on Kant' in Lyotard, *Le différend*, pp. 232–46 and its reworking in *L'enthousiasme*, pp. 45–77 (see also: *Judicieux dans le différend*, p. 215).

37 Lyotard, *The Postmodern Explained*, p. 96.

38 Lyotard, *Enthusiasm*, p. 63.

39 Lyotard, *Enthusiasm*, pp. 63–64.

40 Lyotard, *Judicieux dans le différend*, p. 200 (translation mine).

41 Lyotard, *Moralités postmodernes*, pp. 79–94, p. 94.

42 Lyotard, *Le postmoderne expliqué aux enfants*, p. 53.

43 Cf. Lyotard, *L'enthousiasme*, p. 81.

44 Lyotard, *Enthusiasm*, p. 67.

45 Lyotard, *Political Writings*, p. 21.

Chapter 3

1 Cf. Lyotard, *Le postmoderne expliqué aux enfants*, pp. 124–25.

2 Lyotard, *Peregrinations*, p. 20.

3 Lyotard, *Political Writings*, p. 28. For the avant-garde in the sciences, he refers, among others, to Paul Feyerabend.

4 Lyotard, *The Postmodern Explained*, p. 80.

5 This chapter is primarily based on the following texts from Lyotard: *Le différend*, especially D192, D256 and *Kant 4* (the latter returns in *L'enthousiasme*: enthusiasm as a sublime feeling); further short references in *Tombeau de l'intellectuel et autres papiers*, resp. 9–22, 67–73, and 75–87, and in *Judicieux dans le différend*, pp. 195–200; a more detailed treatment in *Le postmoderne expliqué aux enfants*, resp. 11–34, 105–15 and 117–26; in *L'inhumain*, resp. 33–55, 89–99, 101–17, 119–29, 131–39 and 147–55; in *Pérégrinations*, pp. 61–66, 79–84; and also in *Moralités postmodernes*, 185–98 and 199–210. A specific reflection on Kant's aesthetics is offered in *Leçons sur l'Analytique dus sublime*.

6 The terminology of the 'sublime' or the 'exalted' comes from Boileau who in 1674 translated a text of a certain Longinus (*Peri tou hupsou*), situated around the end of the first century. For more information and a commentary, see Lyotard, *L'inhumain*, pp. 105–9.

7 Lyotard, *The Postmodern Explained*, p. 10.

8 Cf. Lyotard, *Leçons sur l'Analytique du sublime*, p. 74. Compare Lyotard, *Moralités postmodernes*, p. 203.

9 Lyotard, *L'inhumain*, p. 98.

10 Cf. Lyotard, *L'inhumain*, p. 148; Lyotard says he borrowed the words 'quasi perceptible', and likewise 'negative presentation', from Kant, without indicating where he found them. In this context, Kant also ventured to speculate on the Old Testament prohibition on any images of God as the example par excellence of a negative presentation ('negative Darstellung') (in this regard, see: Lyotard, *L'inhumain*, p. 110; for Kant: *Kritik der Urteilskraft* (Hamburg: Meiner, 1974), pp. 122–23.

11 Cf. Lyotard, *L'inhumain*, p. 149.

12 As developed in the *Philosophical Enquiry into the Origin of Our Ideas of the Sublime and the Beautiful* (1757), an aesthetics which is partly adopted, partly rejected by Kant. For a more detailed treatment, see Lyotard, *L'inhumain*, pp. 95–96 and 110–12. See also Lyotard, *Moralités postmodernes*, pp. 206–7.

13 For Burke, the art of the sublime was poetry, which he deemed capable of deferring aroused anxiety and threat (the phrase that would come no more) in the welcoming of a worded phrase.

14 Lyotard, *The Postmodern Explained*, p. 11. Compare Lyotard, *Moralités postmodernes*, p. 204.

15 Cf. Lyotard's discussion on the work of Barnett Baruch Newman and Cézanne in Lyotard, *L'inhumain*, pp. 101–17 (= *Le sublime et l'avant-garde*). Lyotard translates the title of an essay of Newman's from 1948, 'The Sublime is Now', as: '"now", that is the sublime', whereby he attempts to reproduce the 'now' of the event as a question mark. For Lyotard's commentary on Newman, see likewise *L'inhumain*, pp. 89–99 (= *L'instant, Newman*).

16 Lyotard, *L'inhumain*, p. 112.

17 Cf. Lyotard, *L'inhumain*, p. 112.

18 Lyotard refers to both Nazism, and Liberal and Marxist attempts to contain such an aesthetics of the sublime (resp. Lyotard, *L'inhumain*, pp. 115–16 and 137).

19 Lyotard, *The Postmodern Explained*, p. 15.

20 Lyotard, *Postmodern Fables*, p. 245.

21 Just as the painter in painting refers to unpresentability, the philosopher in writing bears witness to that aspect of heterogeneity which cannot be grasped in phrases. Just as only a plurality of distinct commentaries can refer to that which modern painting is about – whereby these commentaries themselves are 'artworks' insofar as they also substantially refer to that to which the artwork refers – thus the event cannot be articulated in one phrase, as in one discourse, but is testified to by an irreducible plurality of phrases and discourses. 'It seems to me that the only consensus we ought to be worrying about is one that would encourage this heterogeneity or "dissensus"' (Lyotard, *Peregrinations*, p. 44).

Chapter 4

1 Cf. J. Habermas, *Die Moderne – ein unvollendetes Projekt (1980)*, in *Kleine Politische Schriften (I-IV)* (Frankfurt am Main: Suhrkamp, 1981), pp. 444–64.

2 R. Rorty, *Habermas and Lyotard on Postmodernism*, in R. Rorty, *Essays on Heidegger and Others* (Philosophical Papers, 2) (Cambridge: Cambridge University Press, 1991), pp. 164–76, p. 176.

3 Cf. Lyotard, *Le postmoderne expliqué aux enfants*, pp. 13–16. Whether Lyotard does justice to Habermas here can be doubted. Habermas proposes to think rationalization as differentiation (here, of art) but within the framework of the primacy of a reintegrated communicative rationality. If Lyotard wished to criticize Habermas, it is especially this reintegration and the demand for communicability that he should have gone after.

4 For more information, including bibliographical references, about Charles Jencks, see http://www.charlesjencks.com/.

5 Lyotard, *The Postmodern Explained*, p. 8.

6 Lyotard, *The Postmodern Explained*, p. 7.

7 See A. Amaud and J.-F. Lyotard, *Le partage des conséquences*, from *Les immatériaux* (Paris, 1985 [n.p.]).

8 Lyotard, *The Inhuman*, p. 106.

9 For this analysis, see Lyotard, *Tombeau de l'intellectuel et autres papiers*, pp. 41–56.

10 Here Lyotard identifies politics with a particular discourse, which in itself is already problematic, as we saw in Chapter 2.

11 Money counts as accumulated time. For example, a labourer can only make his or her time count for money. In the monetary circuit of investment, loan and saving, time has become a commodity (D246–48), banks speak of the sale of (banking) products.

12 Cf. Lyotard, *Judicieux dans le différend*, p. 235.

13 See, for example, Lyotard, *L'inhumain*, pp. 57–67.

14 Lyotard, *The Inhuman*, p. 54.

15 Lyotard, *The Inhuman*, p. 77. The present techno-scientific complex has completed the Cartesian project: 'devenir maître et possesseur de la nature'. But insofar as the person is also ranked under nature, he/she loses one's mastery over oneself. The domination is complete, but no longer human. In this regard, see Lyotard, *Le postmoderne expliqué aux enfants*, pp. 41–42 and *L'humain*, pp. 13–15.

16 Lyotard, *Postmodern Fables*, pp. 11–12.

17 Cf. Lyotard, *L'inhumain*, pp. 33–44 (= *Réécrire la modernité*). Lyotard explicitly acknowledges Freud for this further on (pp. 64–67).

18 To civilize, understood in this way, 'is assisting the consciousness and the will to operate in the complexity'. Culture then distinguishes itself entirely from the culture industry, where complexity anticipatively enervates the event (quote from: A. Amaud and J.-F. Lyotard, *Le partage des conséquences*, [n.p.] – translation mine).

19 For Lyotard, both Jürgen Habermas and Richard Rorty are representatives hereof. For Habermas communication is a necessary condition for freedom and rationality; for Rorty it is the conditio-sine-qua-non for human solidarity.

20 Cf. Lyotard's reflection regarding human rights in *Moralités postmodernes*, pp. 109–10 and pp. 167–68. Precisely that which per definition is not taken up into the system provides the right to be able to speak of human rights. Human rights must not prompt us to forget that there is something that does not allow itself to be rendered in the rights of the individual or of the community. See also *Moralités postmodernes*, pp. 171–84.

21 Cf. supra (Lyotard, *Moralités postmodernes*, p. 94).

22   Lyotard offers for instance a concentrated look at his own thinking and the
     evolution it has undergone in *Pérégrinations. Loi, forme, événement* (Paris:
     Galilée, 1988), the French edition of the 'Wellek Library Lectures' that he
     delivered in May 1986 at the invitation of the 'Critical Theory Group' of the
     University of California – Irvine (English edition: *Peregrinations: Law, Form,
     Event*, New York: Columbia University Press, 1988).
23   Lyotard, *The Inhuman*, p. 77. See also, among others, *Le postmoderne expli-
     qué aux enfants*, pp. 89–90.
24   Lyotard, *The Inhuman*, p. 103. See also: *Le postmoderne expliqué aux enfants*,
     pp. 115 and 141.
25   From the back flap of Lyotard *L'inhumain* (translation mine).
26   Lyotard, *Lectures d'enfance* (Paris: Galilée, 1991), p. 9 (translation mine).
27   Lyotard, *Lectures d'enfance*, p. 9 (translation mine).
28   Cf. Lyotard, *L'inhumain*, p. 86.

Chapter 5

1   Cf. chapter 2 (for the description of Christianity: Lyotard, *The Postmodern
    Explained*, p. 25).
2   Among other places in Lyotard, see *Le postmoderne expliqué aux enfants*,
    p. 47; *Heidegger et 'les juifs'*, pp. 69–70; and in *Moralités postmodernes*,
    pp. 74, 90 and 182. With regard to the relation between Judaism and Christi-
    anity (and the dialectical sublation of Judaism in the latter), see J.-F. Lyotard
    and E. Grüber, *Un trait d'union* (Sainte-Foy: Le Griffon d'argile, 1993) (ET:
    Lyotard and Gruber, *The Hyphen: Between Judaism and Christianity*, New
    York: Humanity Books, 1999).
3   Lyotard, *The Differend*, D232.
4   In *Moralités postmodernes* (p. 74), Lyotard indicates Paul of Tarsus as the
    most important protagonist of the primordial role of the theme of love.
5   Lyotard, *The Differend*, D235.
6   Lyotard, *The Differend*, D235.
7   Lyotard, *Postmodern Fables*, p. 96.
8   Lyotard, *Postmodern Fables*, pp. 97–98.
9   Lyotard, *The Differend*, D232.
10 Lyotard, *The Differend*, D233.
11 Lyotard, *The Differend*, D235.
12 Lyotard, *The Differend*, D233.

Chapter 6

1   Lyotard, *The Differend*, D234. See also, Davis, *St Lyotard*, pp. 127–28.
2   Lyotard, *The Differend*, D234.

3   Lyotard, *The Differend*, D234.
4   Lyotard, *Postmodern Fables*, p. 121.
5   Lyotard, *Postmodern Fables*, p. 213. See also his *La Confession d'Augustin*, and our comments *infra* in this regard.
6   Cf. Lyotard, *Heidegger et 'les juifs'*, pp. 43–48, 65–66, 69–70, 71–73 (ET: Lyotard, *Heidegger and 'the jews'*, pp. 21–23, 34–35, 38, 39–40). About 'the jews', Lyotard explains: 'I use quotation marks to avoid confusing these "jews" with real Jews. What is most real about real Jews is that Europe, in any case, does not know what to do with them: Christians demand their conversion; monarchs expel them; republics assimilate them; Nazis exterminate them' (Lyotard, *Heidegger and 'the jews'*, p. 3).
7   Lyotard, *Heidegger and 'the jews'*, pp. 34–35.
8   This same point arises when Lyotard speaks about the preacher. He proclaims the good news of the word that became flesh. He 'pre-dicts' (pre-dicare: to preach); he says what has been 'pre-dicted' to him. Because the word has become flesh, the preacher needs to bear witness to this grace here and now. But how? 'How this is possible is a Christian question. And the response is Christian, purely Christian: that there is no how that can be mastered, no *technè* to preach, but that it needs grace descended into the mouth, which pre-dicates (*pré-dit*). Descended once more' (Lyotard, *Heidegger and 'the jews'*, p. 38).
9   Lyotard, *Heidegger and 'the jews'*, p. 38.
10 Cf. Lyotard, *Heidegger et 'les juifs'*, pp. 71–73.
11 Cf. J.-F. Lyotard, *D'un trait d'union*, in Lyotard and Gruber, *Un trait d'union. Suivi de Un trait, ce n'est pas tout et Lettre*, pp. 23–44.
12 Lyotard and Gruber, *The Hyphen: Between Judaism and Christianity*, p. 15.
13 Lyotard and Gruber, *The Hyphen: Between Judaism and Christianity*, p. 24.
14 Lyotard and Gruber, *The Hyphen: Between Judaism and Christianity*, p. 25.
15 Cf. Lyotard, *Moralités postmodernes*, pp. 74–75. We already used this mention of Christianity to illustrate Lyotard's description of Christianity as the master narrative of love.
16 Lyotard, *Postmodern Fables*, p. 78.
17 Lyotard, *Heidegger and the 'jews'*, p. 34.
18 Cf. Lyotard, *L'inhumain*, p. 86 (ET: *The Inhuman: Reflections on Time*), p. 74: 'In the very heart of Western culture, such an attitude has, or had, its analogue in the manner of being and thinking which issued from the Judaic tradition. What this tradition calls "study" and "reading" requires that any reality be treated as an obscure message addressed by an unknowable or even unnameable agency.'
19 At the same time, 'the jews' bear witness to the fact that there is always a forgetting going on. They are the people of the Law – the Law not to forget. 'The thought of Heidegger is completely focused on remembering that there is forgetfulness in all philosophy, in every representation, in all politics. A forgetfulness of Being. How has it been possible that this has lent itself to national-socialist politics? How could it forget, ignore until the end, the extermination of those who remember the Forgotten' (Lyotard, *Heidegger et 'les juifs'*, back cover, translation mine).
20 Cf. Lyotard, *Le postmoderne expliqué aux enfants*, pp. 54–55.

21 Cf. resp. D. Janicaud, *Le tournant théologique dans la phenoménologie française* (Combas: Éclat, 1991); H. de Vries, *Philosophy and the Turn to Religion* (Baltimore: The Johns Hopkins University Press, 1999).

22 For a critical presentation, and theological evaluation, see my *Theological Truth in the Context of Contemporary Continental Thought: The Turn to Religion and the Contamination of Language*, in F. Depoortere and M. Lambkin (eds), *The Question of Theological Truth: Philosophical and Interreligious Perspectives* (Currents of Encounter, 46) (Amsterdam: Rodopi, 2012), pp. 77–100; further also my *God, Particularity and Hermeneutics. A Critical-Constructive Theological Dialogue with Richard Kearney on Continental Philosophy's Turn (in)to Religion*, in *Ephemerides Theologicae Lovanienses* 81 (2005), pp. 305–33.

23 Cf. J. Derrida, *Comment ne pas parler? Dénégations*, in Derrida, *Psychè. Inventions de l'autre* (Paris: Galilée, 1987), pp. 535–95; *Sauf le nom* (Paris: Galilée, 1993).

24 Cf. J.-F. Lyotard, *La Confession d'Augustin* (Paris: Galilée, 1998) (ET: *The Confession of Augustine*, Stanford: Stanford University Press, 2000).

25 See J. Derrida, *Circumfession*, in G. Bennington and J. Derrida, *Jacques Derrida* (Paris: Editions de Seuil, 1991), 7–291; and its further discussion in J. Caputo and M. Scanlon (eds), *Augustine and Postmodernism: Confessions and Circumfession* (Bloomington and Indianapolis: Indiana University Press, 2005).

26 Lyotard, *The Confession of Augustine*, p. 36.

27 J. Caputo, *Shedding Tears Beyond Being. Derrida's Confession of Prayer*, in Caputo and Scanlon (eds), *Augustine and Postmodernism*, pp. 95–114, p. 103.

28 Hinting at this, Jean Bethke Elshtain writes in her contribution to *Augustine and Postmodernism*: 'Augustine, in fact, anticipates postmodern strategies in dethroning the Cartesian subject even before that subject got erected. For Augustine, the mind can never be transparent to itself, we are never wholly in control of our thoughts; . . . we know that we exist, not because "I think therefore I am", but rather, "I doubt, therefore I know I exist". Only a subject who is a self that can reflect on itself can doubt. His *Confessions* is a story of a human being who has become a question to himself' (*Why Augustine? Why Now?*, in Caputo and Scanlon (eds), *Augustine and Postmodernism*, 244–56, p. 246).

29 Cf. R. Dodaro, *Loose Canons. Augustine and Derrida on Their Selves*, in Caputo and Scanlon (eds), *Augustine and Postmodernism*, pp. 79–111. This point is, following Dodaro, also taken up by W. J. Hankey in his *Re-Christianizing Augustine Postmodern Style. Readings by Jacques Derrida, Robert Dodaro, Jean-Luc Marion, Rowan Williams, Lewis Ayres and John Milbank*, in *Animus: A Philosophical Journal for our Time* 2 (1997), pp. 1–34 – cf. http://www.swgc.mun.ca/animus/1997vol2/hankey1.htm.

30 Richard Kearney especially would criticize Lyotard in this regard. In *Strangers, Gods and Monsters*, Kearney points to the dangerous move Lyotard makes, for example, when attributing the 'same model of the sublime to the unspeakable horror of the Holocaust and the equally unspeakable alterity of the Hebrew Lord': 'any equivalence between the unspeakability of the Most High Lord (*makom*) and the unspeakability of abyssal evil (*privatio boni*) must

[. . .] give room for pause. If the divine becomes sublime to the point of becoming sadism it has, in my view, ceased to be divine' (R. Kearney, *Strangers, Gods and Monsters: Interpreting Otherness*, London: Routledge, 2003, p. 95).

31 In the same vein Frances Young pointed out the difference between Augustine and postmodern thought when discussing the (too facile) claim that Augustine's sign theory and hermeneutics would be precursors of postmodern literary criticism. From the comparison of Augustine's hermeneutics with postmodern hermeneutics she concluded that ultimately the theological starting point of the Church Father relativizes language and the self: 'We mortals no longer make judgements about truth and meaning; rather, the truth and meaning of God judges us and transforms us.' Augustine is not merely concerned with signs, and the play of signs, but with God as the ultimate referent of the Bible. And she concludes: 'Augustine must be rescued from postmodern critics who think otherwise' (cf. F. Young, *Augustine's Hermeneutics and Postmodern Criticism*, in *Interpretation* 58 (2004), pp. 42–55, resp. pp. 54 and 55).

32 See also Lyotard, *Le postmoderne expliqué aux enfants*, p. 53.

33 See, for example, J.-L. Marion, *Dieu sans l'être* (Paris: Communio/Fayard, 1982); L.-M. Chauvet, *Symbole et sacrement. Une relecture sacramentelle de l'existence chrétienne* (Paris: Cerf, 1987).

34 This calls, as it were, for the same exercise Kevin Hart engaged in when he inquired into what way Jacques Derrida's thinking could inspire theology today. Cf. K. Hart, *The Trespass of the Sign* (Cambridge: Cambridge University Press, 1989, 2nd edn, 2000).

35 For this see my *God, Particularity and Hermeneutics*; and my: *Theological Truth, Particularity and Incarnation: Engaging Religious Plurality and Radical Hermeneutics*, in M. Lamberigts, L. Boeve and T. Merrigan (eds), *Orthodoxy: Process and Product* (BETL, 227) (Leuven: Peeters Press, 2009), pp. 323–48.

Chapter 7

1 We hinted at this image already in Chapter 2.

2 Cf. Lyotard, *Le différend*, pp. 189–93 (= Kant Notice 3); *L'enthousiasme*, p. 3144. We make use here of the most recent version in *L'enthousiasme*.

3 As in the previous chapters, it is not our intention to investigate the correctness of Lyotard's reception of Kant. We only want to sketch here the background in order to understand Lyotard's image of the archipelago.

4 For Lyotard, these faculties are potentials of well-formed phrases, that is answering to specific rules of formation and presentation. These phrases are indeed evaluated as valid when an appropriated object can be presented warranting this claim of validity.

5 Lyotard, *Enthusiasm*, pp. 12–13.

6 Lyotard, *Enthusiasm*, p. 19.

7 In another place in *L'enthousiasme*, Lyotard makes the distinction between 'famille de phrases' and 'genre de discours'; in other words, 'famille de

phrases' functions as a synonym for 'régime de phrases' (p. 89). And on p. 111 he explicitly speaks of 'une "mer", celle où l'archipel des phrases est dispersé' ('a "mer" [sea], the one in which the archipelago of phrases is dispersed' [Lyotard, *Enthusiasm*, p. 65]), after which he declares a bit further that the sea stands for the linking (and linking is something happening between phrases).

8   See W. Welsch, *Vernunft im Übergang*, in W. Reese-Schäfer and B. H. F. Taureck (eds), *Jean-François Lyotard* (Denker des 20. Jahrhunderts, 2) (Cuxhaven: Junghans, 1989), pp. 1–38, p. 19: 'Die Kantischen Vernunftarten bzw. die Lyotardschen Diskursarten (die er hier "Satzfamilien" nennt) sind klar voneinander getrennt wie Inseln' (= W. Welsch, *Vernunft. Die zeitgenössische Vernunftskritik und das Konzept der transversalen Vernunft*, Frankfurt am Main: Suhrkamp, 1995), p. 330.

9   Welsch briefly refers to Rorty in *Vernunft im Übergang*, p. 29; in the same place he also mentions that Samuel Weber provides a similar critique in S. Weber, *Afterword: Literature – Just Making It*, in J.-F. Lyotard and J.-L. Thébaut (eds), *Just Gaming* (Minneapolis: University of Minnesota Press, 1985), pp. 101–20. Welsch is mistaken, however, in that Weber pays attention in this article to the conclusion that Lyotard himself in his positing of the heterogeneity between phrase regimens and discourse genres again unfolds an extremely prescriptive discourse; Weber does not open fire on the archipelago-model as such.

10 Originally published in French in *Critique* 28 (1985) nr. 456, and republished in R. Rorty, *Objectivity, Relativism, and Truth* (Philosophical Papers, 1) (Cambridge: Cambridge University Press, 1991), pp. 211–22 – we make use of this latest publication.

11 The origin of *L'enthousiasme* lies in a text Lyotard wrote for a lecture he gave in 1981 to the 'Centre de recherche philosophique sur le politique' of Philippe Lacoue-Labarthe and Jean-Luc Nancy. Sections of this text have already appeared in previous publications.

12 Cf. Lyotard, *Le différend*, p. 190; *L'enthousiasme*, p. 33 (italics mine). What is crucial for our problematic is then Lyotard's remark, written in his introductory *Avertissement* (in *L'enthousiasme*, pp. 9–10), that with an eye to the publication of *L'enthousiasme*, he has completely looked through and corrected the original text: 'As for the current edition, the only one that is complete, the initial text has been entirely revised, though in conformity with the spirit that guided it when I wrote it, during 1980–81, while preparing *The Differend*' (Lyotard, *Enthusiasm*, p. 10). With regard to the explanation of the archipelago-image, however, the text of *L'enthousiasme* deviates in a remarkable way from that of *Le différend*.

13 Lyotard, *Enthusiasm*, p. 11.

14 Lyotard, *The Differend*, p. xii.

15 Welsch remarkably does so, even against his own intention; see *Vernunft im Übergang*, p. 18 note 25.

16 This is indeed the way in which Welsch reads Lyotard, and consequently develops his own position defining the postmodern condition as the condition of radical plurality, rather than radical heterogeneity, in W. Welsch, *Unsere postmoderne Moderne* (Weinheim: VCH, 1987).

17 See Welsch, *Vernunft im Übergang*, p. 17: 'Die[se] Grundsituation des Wider-
streits hat zur Folge, daß keine Verkettung eine schlechthin gute, sondern stets
zugleich eine arbiträre und unterdrückende ist' (italics mine).

18 Lyotard, *Enthusiasm*, p. 65 (italics mine).

19 See our earlier comments in Chapter 2 on enthusiasm as a sign of history in
Kant: in the eyes of the German philosopher the enthusiasm that the French
Revolution aroused among observers testified to moral progress in history.

20 We mentioned already, for example, that, for Lyotard, the Christian narrative immediately typifies the event as the experience of divine love, and that
contemporary economic discourse either excludes the event by anticipation or
strives to include it as an article of consumption.

21 Lyotard, *Postmodern Fables*, p. 82.

22 Cf. Lyotard, *Une fable postmoderne*, in *Moralités postmodernes*, pp. 79–94.

23 Cf. 2.2., in reference to Lyotard, *Le différend*, D23–27.

24 A similar distinction, at least between what we called 'Differend 1' and 'Differend 2', is made by Frans van Peperstraten in *Oordeel – oorsprong. Lyotard
tussen Kant en Heidegger*, in *Tijdschrift voor filosofie* 65 (1994), pp. 14–36.

25 Cf. Lyotard, *Peregrinations*, pp. 43–44 (p. 44: 'It seems to me that the only
consensus we ought to be worrying about is one that would encourage this
heterogeneity or "dissensus"').

26 Cf. L. Boeve, *Interrupting Tradition. An Essay on Christian Faith in a Postmodern Context* (Louvain Theological and Pastoral Monographs, 30) (Leuven: Peeters / Grand Rapids: Eerdmans, 2003); *God Interrupts History:
Theology in a Time of Upheaval* (New York: Continuum, 2007).

27 Johann Baptist Metz was one of the first to define 'religion as interruption', and
subsequently profiled this notion as one of the core concepts of his political
theology. For our critical-appreciative engagement with Metz, see Chapter 10.

28 In short, our thesis has been that the contextual interruption of Christian
theology in Europe leads to a theology of interruption. The challenges to
Christianity put forward by the current context stirs Christianity to reconsider
its own interruptive dynamics and identity; and it is precisely a further elaboration of this interruptive dynamics which re-establishes both the contextual
and theological plausibility and the relevance of the Christian faith.

29 On the concept of recontextualization, see our short notes in Chapter 1.

30 For this and the following paragraphs, see also Boeve, *Interrupting Tradition*,
chapter 6.

31 For this and the following paragraphs, see also Boeve, *God Interrupts History*,
chapter 2.

32 See Boeve, *Interrupting Tradition*, chapter 6.

33 Especially in *Interrupting Tradition* (chapter 7) I developed how in his life,
words and deeds, Jesus of Nazareth taught us to recognize this Other God
as interrupting Love. However, it was only the experience of the resurrection – that is the experience of faith that God has reopened the closed and
bloody narrative of Jesus – which led the first witnesses to proclaim Jesus
as the Christ and to make him the normative perspective for their lives. The
Christian tradition is, in essence, nothing more than the historical development, from context to context, of this perspective on the relationship between
humanity and God.

Chapter 8

1 Also the basic tenor of John Paul II's encyclical *Fides et Ratio* would seem to support such a view, although a careful reader may perceive in passing more room to engage postmodern thought than at first sight seems possible (see L. Boeve, *The Swan or the Dove? Two Keys for Reading Fides et Ratio*, in *Philosophy and Theology* 12 (2000), pp. 1, 3–24).

2 Cf. S. Wendel, *Jean-François Lyotard. Ästhetisches Ethos* (München: W. Fink, 1997).

3 Cf. S. Wendel, *Ästhetik des Erhabenen – Ästhetische Theologie? Zur Bedeutung des Nicht-Darstellbaren bei Jean-François Lyotard*, in W. Lesch and G. Schwind (eds), *Das Ende der alten Gewißheiten: theologische Auseinandersetzungen mit der Postmoderne* (Mainz: Grünewald, 1993), pp. 48–72. She has elaborated on the feasibility of a 'postmodern theology' in a similar fashion in *Postmoderne Theologie? Zum Verhältnis von christlicher Theologie und postmoderner Philosophie*, in H. Müller (ed.), *Fundamentaltheologie: Fluchtlinien und gegenwärtige Herausforderungen* (Regensburg: Pustet, 1998), pp. 193–214.

4 Wendel, *Ästhetik des Erhabenen – Ästhetische Theologie?*, p. 58. The translation of this and the following quotes from this article are mine.

5 Wendel, *Ästhetik des Erhabenen – Ästhetische Theologie?*, p. 59.

6 Cf. Wendel, *Ästhetik des Erhabenen – Ästhetische Theologie?*, p. 62.

7 Wendel, *Ästhetik des Erhabenen – Ästhetische Theologie?*, p. 63.

8 In reference to Lyotard, *La condition postmoderne*, pp. 98–99.

9 We cite this important thesis: 'Christian tradition defines God, with reference to metaphysical thinking, on the one hand, as Origin and Creator, transcending the immanence of the world, and, on the other, as Trinity, and therefore as Difference, be it a triune of Unity. From this follows that Lyotard's non-presentable, which one definitely can not perceive as transcendent, original Unity, is simply in contradiction with the concept of God in traditional theological thinking' (Wendel, *Ästhetik des Erhabenen – Ästhetische Theologie?*, pp. 64–65).

10 Wendel, *Ästhetik des Erhabenen – Ästhetische Theologie?*, pp. 65–66.

11 Aside from Kant's *Kritik der Urteilskraft*, Wendel also refers to *Die Religion innerhalb der Grenzen der bloßen Vernunft*.

12 Wendel, *Ästhetik des Erhabenen – Ästhetische Theologie?*, p. 68.

13 Cf. Wendel, *Ästhetik des Erhabenen – Ästhetische Theologie?*, p. 68.

14 Wendel, *Ästhetik des Erhabenen – Ästhetische Theologie?*, p. 69.

15 Wendel, *Ästhetik des Erhabenen – Ästhetische Theologie?*, p. 71.

16 For this claim, see Lyotard, *Peregrinations*, p. 20, quoted in Chapter 3.

17 Cf. Lyotard, *Le différend*, D190. Also in our model of the open narrative, narratives are to be situated in the historico-political field, where religions profile themselves par excellence as narratives.

18 It should not be surprising that after 1989, because the then accepted Marxist critical consciousness has lost its plausibility, liberation theologians have been challenged to further their recontextualization and to look for new forms of contemporary critical consciousness. Cf. among others, F. Betto, *Did*

Liberation Theology Collapse with the Berlin Wall?, in *Theology Today* 41 (1994), pp. 109–12; D. B. Forrester, *Can Liberation Theology Survive 1989*, in *Scottish Journal of Theology* 47 (1994), pp. 245–53. For a serious attempt in this regard, see R. Fornet Betancourt, *Filosofía intercultural* (Subsidios didácticos, 3; Mexico, 1994); and G. De Schrijver (ed.), *Liberation Theologies on Shifting Grounds. A Clash of Socio-Economic and Cultural Paradigms* (BETL, 135) (Leuven: Peeters, 1998).

19 See R. Schaeffler, *Religion und kritisches Bewußtsein* (Freiburg: Alber, 1973).

20 Together with Kurt Feyaerts, I have developed this further in *Religious Metaphors in a Postmodern Culture. Transverse Links between Apophatical Theology and Cognitive Semantics*, in L. Boeve and K. Feyaerts (eds), *Metaphor and God-talk* (Religions and Discourse, 2) (Bern: Peter Lang, 1999), pp. 153–84.

Chapter 9

1 For a more extensive elaboration thereof, see L. Boeve, *Post-Modern Sacramento-Theology: Retelling the Christian Story*, in *Ephemerides Theologicae Lovanienses* 74 (1998), pp. 326–43.

2 That this could be the case for Thomas Aquinas follows from the study of F. O'Rourke, *Pseudo-Dionysius and the Metaphysics of Aquinas* (Leiden: Brill, 1992).

3 Thomas Aquinas, *Summa theologiae*, Ia, q. 13, art. 5, ed. Blackfriars in conjunction with London, Eyre & Spottiswoode / New York: McGraw-Hill, vol. 3, trans. H. McCabe, 1964, p. 53.

4 G. De Schrijver, *Experiencing the Sacramental Character of Existence: Transitions from Premodernity to Modernity, Postmodernity, and the Rediscovery of the Cosmos*, in J. Lamberts (ed.), *Current Issues in Sacramental Theology* (Leuven: Abdij Keizersberg / Faculteit Godgeleerdheid, 1994), pp. 12–27, p. 13.

5 This point is worked out in L.-M. Chauvet, *Symbole et sacrement. Une relecture sacramentelle de l'existence chrétienne* (Paris: Cerf, 1990), esp. pp. 13–49 (chapter 1: 'Critique des présupposés onto-théologiques de la sacramentaire classique'); ET: *Symbol and Sacrament: A Sacramental Reinterpretation of Christian Existence* (Collegeville: Liturgical Press, 1995), pp. 7–45.

6 Thomas Aquinas, *Summa theologiae*, III, q. 62, art. 1 (cf. n. 6, vol. 56, trans. D. Bourke, 1975, p. 53). See also art. 2: 'considered in itself grace perfects the essence of the soul in virtue of the fact that this participates, by way of a kind of likeness, in the divine being. And just as it is from the essence of the soul that its powers flow, so too it is from grace that there flow into the powers of the soul certain perfections called the virtues and Gifts, by which those powers are perfected so as to achieve a further fulfillment in the acts proper to them' (p. 58). Thomas continues that *sacramental* grace adds something over and above the grace of the virtues and the Gifts, 'namely a special kind of divine assistance to help in attaining the end of the sacrament concerned' (p. 59).

7   Cf. Thomas Aquinas, *Summa theologiae*, pp. 53–54: 'this is the way in which the sacraments of the New Law cause grace. For it is by divine institution that they are conferred upon man for the precise purpose of causing grace in and through them.. . . Now the term "instrument" in its true sense is applied to that through which someone produces an effect'.

8   Cf. H. U. von Balthasar, *Herrlichkeit. Eine theologische Ästhetik. Fächer der Stile* (Einsiedeln: Johannes, 1962); *Herrlichkeit. Eine theologische Ästhetik. Im Raum von Metaphysik* (Einsiedeln: Johannes, 1965).

9   See, for example, J. Ratzinger, *Theologische Prinzipienlehre. Bausteine zur Fundamentaltheologie* (München: Wewel, 1982).

10 J. Ratzinger, *Die sakramentale Begründung christlicher Existenz* (Meitinger Kleinschriften) (Freising: Kyrios, 2nd edn, 1967), pp. 18–19 (translation mine).

11 Ratzinger, *Die sakramentale Begründung*, p. 19.

12 Cf., for example, K. Rahner, *Grundkurs des Glaubens. Einführung in den Begriff des Christentums* (Freiburg/Basel/Wien: Herder, 1976), pp. 35–36 (ET: *Foundations of Christian Faith. An Introduction to the Idea of Christianity*, New York: Crossroad, 1984).

13 Rahner, *Foundations of Christian Faith*, p. 121. In the next paragraph Rahner situates the ontological foundation and legitimation in the transcendental experience of every finite being towards the absolute being and mystery of God. As such, transcendence, in a first movement towards the creature, underpins the transcendental movement towards transcendence.

14 K. Rahner, *Foundations of Christian Faith*, p. 390. On the sacrament as 'real symbol', see *Überlegungen zum personalen Vollzug des sakramentalen Geschehens*, in *Schriften zur Theologie*, Bd. X (Einsiedeln/Zürich/Köln: Benzinger Verlag, 1972), pp. 405–29, esp. pp. 422–23. Rahner here attempts to revise the causality-model in which the sacraments have been conceived ('sacraments cause what they signify'): the grace for which the sacrament stands is distinguished precisely where the individual person takes up the freedom and free choice which God has bequeathed to him or her, such that he or she is thus brought to the fullness of human personhood.

15 We refer here, among others, to the work of Edward Schillebeeckx (e.g. *Gerechtigheid en liefde. Genade en bevrijding*, Bloemendaal: Nelissen, 1977) and Johann-Baptist Metz (*Glaube in Geschichte und Gesellschaft. Studien zu einer praktischen Fundamentaltheologie*, Mainz: Matthias Grünewald, 1977).

16 E. Schillebeeckx, *Christ. The Experience of Jesus as Lord* (New York: Crossroad, 1989), p. 836.

17 J.-L. Marion, *Dieu sans l'être* (Paris: Communio/Fayard, 1982); *Etant donné: essai d'une phénoménologie de la donation* (Paris: Presses Universitaires de France 1997).

18 Chauvet, *Symbole et sacrament*, especially part 1. For critical-constructive engagements with Chauvet's proposals, see P. Bordeyne and B. T. Morill (eds), *Sacraments Revelation of the Humanity of God: Engaging the Fundamental Theology of Louis-Marie Chauvet* (Collegeville: Liturgical Press, 2008), pp. 5–23.

19 Chauvet, *Symbole et sacrament*, pp. 78–79.

Chapter 10

1   In this way we are engaging in an attempt at continuing Metz's own project
    of 'Korrektivtheologie', which he defines as developing a critical-constructive
    theology which 'understands itself as a corrective with respect to existing theo-
    logical projects and systems, and – in a critical-corrective relationship with the
    latter – saves and passes on the content and intention thereof' (Metz, *Glaube
    in Geschichte und Gesellschaft*, p. 12).

2   Originally in Metz, *Glaube in Geschichte und Gesellschaft*, p. 150, thesis vi;
    also mentioned in *Unterbrechungen. Theologisch-politische Perspektiven und
    Profile* (Gütersloh: Gütersloher Taschenbücher Siebenstern, 1981), p. 86. For
    Metz's theology, see further the collection of excerpts and articles by Metz that
    traces the evolution of his Ideas: *Zum Begriff der neuen Politischen Theologie*
    (Mainz: Grünewald, 1997).

3   J. B. Metz, *Faith in History and Society: Towards a Practical Fundamental
    Theology* (New York: Seabury Press, 2007), p. 158. The other translations of
    German citations further in this chapter are mine.

4   Another personal experience during World War II seems to have had the same
    effect on his theological and spiritual position: Almost at the end of the war,
    Johann Baptist Metz, only 16 years old, was forced to join the army and was
    sent to the front to stop the allied forces from conquering Germany. One
    evening, his company commander commissioned him with a message to be
    brought to the headquarters of the battalion. When, however, the following
    morning Metz returned to his post, he found all his companions dead, nobody
    had survived the combined air and tank attack of that night. About this expe-
    rience, he writes: 'I remember nothing but a soundless cry ("nichts als einen
    lautlosen Schrei"). That is the way I still see myself today, and behind this
    memory all the dreams of my childhood have fallen away . . . Up until today
    my prayers are fulfilled with this soundless cry. And my theological work
    is – and the older I become, the more insistent – characterised by a special
    sensibility for the so-called theodicy question, for the question for God in light
    of the unfathomable history of suffering of the world, which though should be
    "his" world': J. B. Metz, *Memoria Passionis. Ein Provozierendes Gedächtnis in
    pluralistischer Gesellschaft* (Freiburg: Herder, 2006), p. 94.

5   Cf. *Welches Christentum hat Zukunft? Dorothee Sölle und Johann Baptist
    Metz im Gespräch mit Karl-Joseph Kuschel* (Stuttgart: Kreuz-Verlag, 1990),
    p. 23.

6   Metz severely criticizes modernity's identification of emancipation with the
    liberation of the self. The promises that evoke such a concept of 'emancipa-
    tion' simply cannot be fulfilled; the human history of liberation has resulted
    in enormous contradictions. Cf. Metz, *Glaube in Geschichte und Gesellschaft*,
    pp. 114–27.

7   Metz, *Glaube in Geschichte und Gesellschaft*, p. 25.

8   Metz, *Glaube in Geschichte und Gesellschaft*, pp. 208–9.

9   For these reflections, see in particular the contributions Metz published
    after 1985, among others: *Wohin is Gott, wohin denn der Mensch?*, in F.-X.

Kaufmann and J. B. Metz, *Zukunftsfähigkeit. Suchbewegungen im Christentum* (Freiburg: Herder, 1987), pp. 124–47; *Wider die zweite Unmündigkeit*, in J. Rüsen, E. Lämmert and P. Glotz (eds), *Die Zukunft der Aufklärung* (Frankfurt am Main: Suhrkamp, 1988), pp. 81–87; *Anamnetische Vernunft. Anmerkungen eines Theologen zur Krise der Geisteswissenschaften*, in A. Honneth et al. (eds), *Zwischenbetrachtungen. Im Prozeß der Aufklärung* (Fs. J. Habermas) (Frankfurt am Main: Suhrkamp, 1989), pp. 733–38; *Theologie versus Polymythie oder Kleine Apologie des biblischen Monotheismus*, in O. Marquard (ed.), *Einheit und Vielheit. XIV. Deutscher Kongreß für Philosophie* (Hamburg: Meiner, 1990), pp. 170–86; *Religion, ja – Gott, nein*, in J. B. Metz and T. R. Peters, *Gottespassion. Zur Ordensexistenz heute* (Freiburg: Herder, 1991), pp. 11–62; *Gotteskrise*, in J. B. Metz et al., *Diagnosen zur Zeit* (Düsseldorf: Patmos, 1994), pp. 76–92; and various contributions from *Zum Begriff der neuen Politischen Theologie* (1927–97), among others, pp. 149–55 (1997), pp. 156–59 (1994–96), pp. 174–92 (1995–97), pp. 192–96 (1997). Many of these contributions have been integrated into *Memoria passionis*.

10   Cf. Metz, *Religion, ja – Gott, nein*, p. 24: 'Religion today appears to be only Dionysian, as the striving after happiness by shunning suffering and sorrow and by putting at ease erring fears. Religion has become a mythical spell of the soul, a psychological-aesthetical assumption of innocence for people who have stopped all eschatological upheaval in a dream of the return of the same, or . . . in the newly rising phantasies about transmigration of souls and reincarnation.'

11   Cf. J. B. Metz, *Im Eingedenken fremden Leids. Zu einer Basiskategorie christlicher Gottesrede*, in J. B. Metz et al., *Gottesrede* (Religion – Geschichte – Gesellschaft, 1) (Münster: LIT, 1996), pp. 3–20.

12   Cf. Metz, *Zum Begriff der neuen Politischen Theologie*, p. 198.

13   Metz, *Zum Begriff der neuen Politischen Theologie*, p. 205. For this characteristic constitutive role of religion, Metz refers to, among others, what he describes, following other authors, as the Böckenförde-paradox: the modern constitutional state proceeds from presuppositions, from sources, that it does not itself produce nor is able to guarantee, and which it thus consumes without being able to replenish them again (cf. pp. 138, 180–81).

14   Metz, *Wider die zweite Unmündigkeit*, p. 85.

15   Cf. Metz, *Anamnetische Vernunft*. For Habermas's reaction, see J. Habermas, *Israël und Athen oder: Wem gehört die anamnetische Vernunft?*, in J. B. Metz, *Vom sinnlichen Eindruck zum symbolischen Ausdruck* (Frankfurt am Main: Suhrkamp, 1997), pp. 98–111. For the criticism of Lyotard, see, for example, Metz, *Zum Begriff der neuen Politischen Theologie*, pp. 150–51, and p. 195. Also see Metz, *Wohin is Gott, wohin denn der Mensch?*, p. 141.

16   Cf. among others: Metz, *Theologie versus polymythie*, p. 178; *Theologie als Theodizee*, p. 113; and *Religion, ja – Gott, nein*, pp. 25–30.

17   Cf. Metz, *Theologie versus polymythie*, p. 178: 'According to all important witnesses, Israel – embedded in the life here and now and bound to the world – has never experienced and thought its saving God as a God beyond this world, beyond time, but as the coming of their restricting end . . . God "is" in [God's] coming ("Gott 'ist' im Kommen")'.

18   Metz, *Theologie versus polymythie*, p. 179.

19 Cf. Metz, *Im Eingedenken fremden Leids*, pp. 6–7; *Zum Begriff der neuen Politischen Theologie*, pp. 194–95.

20 On several occasions, Metz distances himself from Ratzinger's conviction that Christianity is the successful synthesis, mediated by Jesus Christ, of the Jewish faith and the Greek spirit. See Metz, *Anamnetische Vernunft*, p. 734; *Theologie als Theodizee?*, pp. 111–12.

21 Metz, in his rejection of the turn to language, is not primarily targeting Lyotard – aside from some very short, secondary references, Metz does not seem to know him – but rather Jürgen Habermas' communicative approach: in Metz's view, the freedom of the subject does not lie in the wealth of the subject's language or faculties of communication.

22 Metz also alludes to this intuition in his later articles, after 1985, but does not really develop it further. See, for example, his *Unterwegs zu einer nachidealistischen Theologie*, in J. Bauer (ed.), *Entwürfe der Theologie* (Graz: Styria, 1985), pp. 203–33; *In Aufbruch zu einer kulturell polyzentrischen Weltkirche*, in F.-X. Kaufmann and J. B. Metz, *Zukunftsfähigkeit. Suchbewegungen im Christentum* (Freiburg: Herder, 1987), pp. 93–123; *Die eine Welt als Herausforderung an das westliche Christentum*, in *Una Sancta* 44 (1989), pp. 314–22; and his contributions to *Concilium* collected in J.-B. Metz and J. Moltmann, *Faith and the Future: Essays on Theology, Solidarity, and Modernity* (Concilium Series) (New York: Maryknoll, 1995), pp. 30–37, 57–65 and 66–71, and two contributions in *Zum Begriff der neuen Politischen Theologie*, pp. 135–41 and 197–206.

Conclusion

1 We hinted at this issue in Chapter 6. For my analysis in this regard: L. Boeve, *Theological Truth in the Context of Contemporary Continental Thought: The Turn to Religion and the Contamination of Language*, in F. Depoortere and M. Lambkin (eds), *The Question of Theological Truth: Philosophical and Interreligious Perspectives* (Currents of Encounter, 46) (Amsterdam: Rodopi, 2012), pp. 77–100.

INDEX